MINIMALISM

----- ❧❦❧❦ -----

2 Manuscripts Declutter And Codependency: Art of organizing your home and simplify life

Chris S Jennings

© Copyright 2019 by Chris S Jennings - All rights reserved.

The follow book is reproduced below with the goal of providing information that is as accurate and reliable as possible. Regardless, purchasing this book can be seen as consent to the fact that both the publisher and the author of this book are in no way experts on the topics discussed within and that any recommendations or suggestions that are made herein are for entertainment purposes only. Professionals should be consulted as needed prior to undertaking any of the action endorsed herein.

This declaration is deemed fair and valid by both the American Bar Association and the Committee of Publishers Association and is legally binding throughout the United States.

Furthermore, the transmission, duplication or reproduction of any of the following work including specific information will be considered an illegal act irrespective of if it is done electronically or in print. This extends to creating a secondary or tertiary copy of the work or a recorded copy and is only allowed with express written consent from the Publisher. All additional right reserved.

The information in the following pages is broadly considered to be a truthful and accurate account of facts and as such any inattention, use or misuse of the information in question by the reader will render any resulting actions solely under their purview. There are no scenarios in which the publisher or the original author of this work can be in any fashion deemed liable for any hardship or damages that may befall them after undertaking information described herein.

Additionally, the information in the following pages is intended only for informational purposes and should thus be thought of as universal. As befitting its nature, it is presented without assurance regarding its prolonged validity or interim quality. Trademarks that are mentioned are done without written consent and can in no way be considered an endorsement from the trademark holder.

Your Free Gift

As a way of saying thank you for your purchase, I wanted to offer you a free bonus e-book called **3 Incredible Life Changing Daily Habits That Can Help You To Heal Any Pain In Your Life**

Download the free ebook here: https://www.subscribepage.com/healing

Are you tired of letting your negative emotions consume you? Life throws a lot of curveballs at us: illness, abandonment, death, heartbreak, injury, the list goes on. We have found 3 scientifically endorsed daily habits that can significantly help you to heal any emotional pain and help take back control for you to start living a more positive life right now.

Listen to this book for free

Do you want to be able to listen to this book whenever you want? Maybe whilst driving to work or running errands. It can be difficult nowadays to sit down and listen to a book. So I am really excited to let you know that this book is available in audio format. What's great is you can get this book for FREE as part of a 30-day audible trial. Thereafter if you don't want to stay an Audible member you can cancel, but keep the book.

Benefits of signing up to audible:
- After the trial, you get 1 free audiobook and 2 free audio originals each month
- Can roll over any unused credits
- Choose from over 425,000 + titles
- Listen anywhere with the Audible app and across multiple devices
- Keep your audiobooks forever, even if you cancel your membership

Click below to get started
Audible US - https://tinyurl.com/yxzgnk4k
Audible UK - https://tinyurl.com/yxdz4ldx
Audible FR - https://tinyurl.com/y68rlwjk
Audible DE - https://tinyurl.com/y4f4nxk3

TABLE OF CONTENTS

DECLUTTER YOUR LIFE

INTRODUCTION..1

CHAPTER 1: THE POWER OF DECLUTTERING 3

You Will Feel a Greater Sense of Vibrancy................................ 3
Your Schedule Will Clear Up, Big Time 4
You Begin To Move Forward In Life.. 6
You Can Address Your Personal Issues...................................... 7
Your Habits Can Be Transformed 8
You Feel More Rested and Less Stressed.................................. 9

CHAPTER 2: DECLUTTERING YOUR MINDSET 11

Identifying Your Core Values...12
Overcoming Procrastination 14
Releasing Negative Thought Patterns 17
Increasing Your Mental Resiliency 18

CHAPTER 3: DECLUTTERING YOUR HOME......................... 21

How to Tackle the Decluttering of your Home 22
Decluttering Your Bedroom 22
   Eliminate Unwanted Clothes...23
   Use Your Hamper 23
   Use Containers to Contain the Clutter.........................23
   Organize Your Closet..24
   Use Minimalistic Decorations 24
Decluttering Your Kitchen..24
   Eliminate the Excess Junk..25
   Keep Your Counters Clear...25
   Use Storage Solutions for Cleaner Drawers and Cupboards..25
   Build a Communications Center 26
   Clean Out Underneath Your Sink...................................26
   Clean Out Your Food Supply..26
Decluttering Your Living Room 26
   Return Everything to Where It Belongs 27

Use A Declutter Basket 27
Organize Your Media Cabinet 27
Minimize Your Decorations 28
DECLUTTERING YOUR BATHROOMS 28
Eliminated Unwanted Products 28
Clean Absolutely Everything Off 29
Use Effective Storage Solutions 29
DECLUTTERING STORAGE 29
Commit To Going through Everything 30
Use Labeled Bins 30
Keep the Space Clean 30

CHAPTER 4: DECLUTTERING YOUR FINANCES 33

MASTERING THE ART OF BUDGETING 34
RELEASING FINANCIAL BURDENS YOU DON'T NEED 36
HAVING WEEKLY SPENDING LIMITS 37
TAKING THE OCCASIONAL CASH FREEZE BREAK 38

CHAPTER 5: DECLUTTERING YOUR RELATIONSHIPS 41

IDENTIFYING CLUTTER IN YOUR SOCIAL CIRCLE 42
REMOVING TOXIC RELATIONSHIPS FROM YOUR LIFE 44
Be Completely Honest From the Start 45
Avoid Playing the Blame Game 45
End the Relationship Completely 46
CLEANING UP YOUR SOCIAL MEDIA 47
BEING MORE PRESENT AT THE MOMENT 48
MAKING TIME FOR THE ONES YOU LOVE 50

CHAPTER 6: HEALTHY HABITS FOR DECLUTTERING 53

TAKE THINGS SLOWLY, THERE IS NO RUSH 53
BE PRACTICAL ABOUT WHAT YOU CAN ACHIEVE 54
DO NOT BE AFRAID TO ASK FOR SUPPORT 55
TAKE BEFORE AND AFTER PHOTOGRAPHS 56
BE COMPASSIONATE WITH YOURSELF 57
MAKE IT A FUN EXPERIENCE 58
USE A QUARANTINE PRACTICE IF YOU NEED TO 59
LOOK AT THE POSITIVE SIDE OF THINGS 60
BEGIN BUILDING MORE POSITIVITY INTO YOUR LIFE 61

CONCLUSION 63

CODEPENDENCY

INTRODUCTION 69

CHAPTER 1: UNDERSTANDING CODEPENDENCY 71

What is Codependency? 71
Characteristics of Codependency...74

CHAPTER 2: TYPES OF CODEPENDENT PERSONALITIES AND BEHAVIOR 79

The Martyr 79
The Savior..80
The Coach..80
The Enabler 81
Behaviors 82
Controlling 82
Enabling 84
People-pleasing 86
Self-denigrating 87
Overreacting.. 88

CHAPTER 3: TRAUMA, HEALING, AND FORGIVENESS..... 91

What causes codependency to develop in the first place?91
Self-awareness and self-acceptance 94
Paths to Recovery 96

CHAPTER 4: BEGINNING TO HEAL 101

Recognizing Unhealthy Behavior Patterns 101
Developing Mindfulness... 103
Learning to Love Yourself 108
Accepting Your Partner 110

CHAPTER 5: CHANGING CODEPENDENT RELATIONSHIPS 115

Developing Empathic Communication 116
Nurturing Mutual Respect 119
Establishing Trust 121

CHAPTER 6: BREAKING THE CYCLE OF CODEPENDENCY 125

WHAT DOES A HEALTHY RELATIONSHIP LOOK LIKE? 126
MAINTAINING A MINDFUL RELATIONSHIP DYNAMIC 128
KNOWING WHEN TO WALK AWAY 129
LIVING THE LIFE YOU WANT TO LIVE 132

CONCLUSION **135**

DECLUTTER YOUR LIFE

How to organize a clean home, a clear mind and be on your way to success

Chris S Jennings

TABLE OF CONTENTS

DECLUTTER YOUR LIFE

INTRODUCTION 1

CHAPTER 1: THE POWER OF DECLUTTERING 3

   You Will Feel a Greater Sense of Vibrancy 3
   Your Schedule Will Clear Up, Big Time 4
   You Begin To Move Forward In Life 6
   You Can Address Your Personal Issues 7
   Your Habits Can Be Transformed 8
   You Feel More Rested and Less Stressed 9

CHAPTER 2: DECLUTTERING YOUR MINDSET 11

   Identifying Your Core Values 12
   Overcoming Procrastination 14
   Releasing Negative Thought Patterns 17
   Increasing Your Mental Resiliency 18

CHAPTER 3: DECLUTTERING YOUR HOME 21

   How to Tackle the Decluttering of your Home 22
   Decluttering Your Bedroom 22
      Eliminate Unwanted Clothes 23
      Use Your Hamper 23
      Use Containers to Contain the Clutter 23
      Organize Your Closet 24
      Use Minimalistic Decorations 24
   Decluttering Your Kitchen 24
      Eliminate the Excess Junk 25
      Keep Your Counters Clear 25
      Use Storage Solutions for Cleaner Drawers and Cupboards 25
      Build a Communications Center 26
      Clean Out Underneath Your Sink 26
      Clean Out Your Food Supply 26
   Decluttering Your Living Room 26
      Return Everything to Where It Belongs 27

- *Use A Declutter Basket* 27
- *Organize Your Media Cabinet* 27
- *Minimize Your Decorations* 28
- DECLUTTERING YOUR BATHROOMS 28
  - *Eliminated Unwanted Products* 28
  - *Clean Absolutely Everything Off* 29
  - *Use Effective Storage Solutions* 29
- DECLUTTERING STORAGE 29
  - *Commit To Going through Everything* 30
  - *Use Labeled Bins* 30
  - *Keep the Space Clean* 30

CHAPTER 4: DECLUTTERING YOUR FINANCES 33

- MASTERING THE ART OF BUDGETING 34
- RELEASING FINANCIAL BURDENS YOU DON'T NEED 36
- HAVING WEEKLY SPENDING LIMITS 37
- TAKING THE OCCASIONAL CASH FREEZE BREAK 38

CHAPTER 5: DECLUTTERING YOUR RELATIONSHIPS 41

- IDENTIFYING CLUTTER IN YOUR SOCIAL CIRCLE 42
- REMOVING TOXIC RELATIONSHIPS FROM YOUR LIFE 44
  - *Be Completely Honest From the Start* 45
  - *Avoid Playing the Blame Game* 45
  - *End the Relationship Completely* 46
- CLEANING UP YOUR SOCIAL MEDIA 47
- BEING MORE PRESENT AT THE MOMENT 48
- MAKING TIME FOR THE ONES YOU LOVE 50

CHAPTER 6: HEALTHY HABITS FOR DECLUTTERING 53

- TAKE THINGS SLOWLY, THERE IS NO RUSH 53
- BE PRACTICAL ABOUT WHAT YOU CAN ACHIEVE 54
- DO NOT BE AFRAID TO ASK FOR SUPPORT 55
- TAKE BEFORE AND AFTER PHOTOGRAPHS 56
- BE COMPASSIONATE WITH YOURSELF 57
- MAKE IT A FUN EXPERIENCE 58
- USE A QUARANTINE PRACTICE IF YOU NEED TO 59
- LOOK AT THE POSITIVE SIDE OF THINGS 60
- BEGIN BUILDING MORE POSITIVITY INTO YOUR LIFE 61

CONCLUSION 63

INTRODUCTION

Congratulations on downloading **Declutter**!

Over the next six chapters, you are going to be guided on a journey of how you can declutter your life and your home one step at a time. This journey can be a trying one, but it is also highly rewarding and stands to offer you many great benefits along the way. From having a stronger sense of mental clarity and wellbeing to feeling better about your home, there are many benefits that you gain when you focus on decluttering your life.

As you go through this journey, I encourage you to really embrace the act of compassion and understanding. The fact that you have chosen to invest in learning more about the process of decluttering proves that you are serious about making meaningful changes in your life. It also suggests that you may have attempted to do it on your own but found that you were left feeling overwhelmed or at a loss for where to start or what to do. This feeling of frustration and confusion is completely natural, and you are not alone in feeling it. In fact, *most* people feel that way when they begin decluttering their lives and homes! Being compassionate and understanding with yourself and not judging yourself for any feelings that may come up along the way will ensure that you are able to continue along with the process of decluttering.

This book has been designed in a step-by-step process, starting with your mind and leading you to the point of decluttering your social circle and friendships. By following this book in the order it has been presented to you with, you can equip yourself with the necessary resources to successfully achieve each successive step. Attempting to do too much at once or skip over steps could result in an increase in overwhelm and a decreased likelihood of successfully achieving your desired results. For that reason, I highly recommend slowing yourself down and taking it easy. There is no rush towards your results, as long as you are making steady and consistent progress. Be patient with yourself.

If you are ready to begin discovering the power of decluttering and are prepared to declutter your life and your house one step at a time, please be sure to enjoy the process along the way!

Chapter 1: The Power of Decluttering

Have you ever cleaned out your junk drawer and felt that intense burst of energy that made you feel positive, uplifted, and inspired? Maybe it was the console in your car or one of the messier shelves in your pantry, but either way, that moment of seeing that once-cluttered space now clean and organized felt *so good.* Do you remember that feeling? That feeling summarizes the power of decluttering and how it can actually help you live a better life; complete with a greater sense of peace, calm, and efficiency.

The power of decluttering is not only in your mind, either. That positive energy you feel when you declutter a messy space actually supports you in experiencing a greater sense of joy, positivity, and abundance in your life overall. There are many positive benefits to decluttering your life, including the physical and non-physical aspects of it. Before we dive into the 'how,' let's take a moment and explore *why* decluttering has such a powerful impact on your life and what it will actually do for you.

You Will Feel a Greater Sense of Vibrancy

When you declutter your space, your inner world becomes a lot more vibrant and this is reflected in your outer world, too. The more harmony that you experience in your home and in your life, the easier it is for you to be present and live in the moment rather than feeling as though you are constantly being distracted by the disharmonies in your life. As a result of your presence, you will feel a greater sense of radiance and vibrancy in your life, allowing you to show up and enjoy living your life with far greater sincerity and joy than ever before.

Decluttering your life allows you to remove blockages and imbalances from your mind and physical space, clearing up room for you to flow more freely. As a result, your ability to flow into places of happiness and non-resistance become far easier, too. You will feel a fresh sense of inner energy that inspires you to magnetize joy and abundance into your life, which will only further boost your happiness.

While decluttering does not guarantee that you will be laughing and smiling every minute of the day, it does help you anchor in a deeper sense of contentment that is far more sustainable and lasting. So, while you may not feel intense and frequent bursts of positive energy, you will feel a greater sense of true happiness that lingers and keeps you feeling happier about life in general.

Your Schedule Will Clear Up, Big Time

The feelings of overwhelm when your life is cluttered are real, and they have a seriously negative impact on your time. When you have an immense amount of clutter in your life, your schedule always appears to be lacking in extra time for you to be able to actually enjoy your life. You likely find yourself losing minutes or even hours, perhaps, without any clear understanding as to why you have lost them. Maybe you think it is because you are lazy or because you lack personal motivation because that 'extra time' seems to disappear with you hiding out on the couch or filling it in with aimless tasks that do not bring you any joy or fulfillment. In reality, you are likely just experiencing feelings of overwhelm that is preventing you from getting up and actually going about your daily life.

See, in your mind, when you have things you *should* be doing that you don't want to be doing, instead of simply not doing them and doing something more fulfilling or enjoyable, you start wasting time. Somewhere in your mind, you say, "well, if I'm not doing what I *should* be doing, then I shouldn't be doing anything fun, either." This is a way that we attempt to justify why we are not getting things done. Often, the lack of achievement also comes along with excuses like "I'm stressed from work," "I had a headache," or "I deserve a day off." In reality, these excuses are only meant to cover up the reality, which was that you felt overwhelmed by the clutter and you had no idea how to tackle it, so instead, you didn't.

When you tackle clutter effectively and remove it from your life completely, your calendar seems to have so much extra time in it. You are no longer trapped in a cycle of procrastinating from tasks that involve managing your clutter and then doing nothing so that you can justify why nothing got done. Instead, you get it done and you begin to experience an inner sense of openness that gives you permission to go enjoy other things in your life such as reading, hanging out with loved ones, or picking up a new hobby.

You Begin To Move Forward In Life

With all of your spare time, it is inevitable that one of the things that you will accomplish with it is the process of actually moving forward in your life. Now that you have nothing and no one physically or mentally holding you back, you can begin investing in the things that are actually going to draw you forward and help you live a better life. You can invest in things like inner healing, releasing unwanted baggage, finding peace, and taking action towards your lifelong goals. As a result of this action, you are able to clear up your inner life even further and make real progress towards achieving everything you wished that you would achieve in your life.

According to many psychologists, clutter often reflects the unresolved business that you are holding onto in your life. When you begin to move the clutter out, you can bring closure to those things and open up room for you to move forward by taking positive risks in your life. Maybe, releasing your clutter and your attachment to the past allows you to move to a new place, travel more, or pursue your dream job. Maybe, it allows you to release friends that no longer resonate with you, or go ahead and get the dog you have always wanted but never brought home for fear of it destroying your clutter. You can start doing new things and taking new adventures without so much fear of what will happen because you are no longer being held back by your clutter.

You Can Address Your Personal Issues

Another branch of clutter that is keeping you attached to unfinished business is that it can prevent you from experiencing full closure from things that you have experienced in the past. When you dig through your mess and begin getting rid of things, you will find that a lot of objects come forward that bring up old memories and remind you of bad experiences, broken dreams, or moments of grief from your life. When you hold onto things that have these types of negative attachments to them, you essentially bury your feelings and avoid having to actively work through them. Every time you encounter these objects in your house, you may feel a pang of sadness or regret, or maybe even anger. So, holding onto them naturally increases the number of negative experiences that you are having. Finding them may be challenging and may resurface old feelings for you, but getting rid of them once and for all will be incredibly helpful in allowing you to move past your challenges and heal from your personal issues.

As you deep clean each room in your house, as well as your mind, your relationships, your finances, and your life in general, you will find that you begin to experience emotional and mental freedom from things that have been hurting you. This will help you move on from these experiences and have closure surrounding them so that you can fully move forward and embrace the next stages of your life. Even though it may be emotional or challenging in the beginning, it will be fulfilling and helpful in the long run. The closure will support you in moving on for good and welcoming newer experiences into your life that brings you more opportunities to enjoy life and grow from your challenges.

Your Habits Can Be Transformed

Keeping yourself surrounded by the same clutter day in and day out can leave you feeling trapped inside of bad habits that have never effectively served you in living a better life. When you work towards decluttering your house and your life, you begin to experience a change from your standard daily routine. This change is often enough to help jolt you out of any bad habits that you have been feeling entrapped in, while also giving you the room that you need to embrace new positive habits.

Another significant way that decluttering is going to help you eliminate bad habits is through helping you release the triggers that exist for those bad habits to transpire in the first place. For example, say that you have been trying to eat healthier but you find yourself always reaching for sugary treats or snacks in-between meals and it has been preventing you from making positive improvements. Maybe you think that you are weak or incapable of change, so instead, you keep justifying why you are going for the sweets, rather than making a larger change that will prevent you from being able to reinforce negative habits. By decluttering, you can choose to remove the sugars and sweets from your house entirely so that the ability to act on your habits is removed and you have to start making different decisions. When you eliminate the triggers from your life, your bad habits have nothing to thrive on so they naturally diminish and leave you with the opportunity to turn to positive habits, instead.

You Feel More Rested and Less Stressed

Clutter is known for generating high feelings of stress in people who are regularly surrounded by it. Having massive amounts of clutter in your space can leave you feeling higher levels of stress for many different reasons, from feeling obligated to do something about it to feeling stressed out that you cannot find anything or that simple tasks are now harder. There are many ways that clutter can significantly increase the amount of stress that you experience, thus making it significantly harder for you to experience calmness and relaxation.

When you are consistently feeling even small amounts of stress in your life, the continual trigger of negative thoughts and emotions can result in increased levels of cortisol and adrenaline in your body. If these hormones are triggered often enough, they can lead to disturbances in your sleep and in your ability to relax in general. People who are surrounded by a lot of clutter often find themselves struggling to fully rest because they feel a continued sense of stress that lingers with them on a daily basis. By removing the clutter that is causing your stress, you can give yourself the opportunity to enter a deeper state of relaxation and feel more at peace in your life. This increased feeling of general peace allows you to begin feeling a greater sense of ease in your life, as well as an increased ability to experience deep and effective relaxation and sleep. As a result, you no longer begin to carry the effects of prolonged stress around because they are eased by peace.

Chapter 2: Decluttering Your Mindset

The first step to decluttering your life is decluttering your mindset. Your mindset is the part of you that allows you to hold on to clutter in your life, justify why you are doing so, and reinforce negative habits that keep the clutter lingering far past its expiration date. When your mindset is not healthy and focused, it is easy for you to put off doing anything about the clutter in your life because facing it feels uncomfortable or challenging.

Decluttering your mindset gives you the opportunity to understand how decluttering your life will improve your quality of living. It also provides you with the opportunity to empower yourself with the resources that you need to embrace and sustain the practice of decluttering the rest of your life. When you are in the right frame of mind, facing the emotions that may arise when it comes to eliminating unwanted or unhelpful items from your life becomes a lot easier. You will also have an easier time giving yourself permission to eliminate toxic people from your life, make financial changes, and embrace the art of decluttered living in general.

In this chapter, we are going to start by identifying how you can get clear on what matters to you and then declutter your mind so that your mental processes reflect your values. That way, you will have an easier time making more permanent physical changes in your life because you will be mentally equipped with the motivation, energy, and resources to do so. It is important that you start with mindset because without it, you may find yourself failing to actively make any changes in your life or struggling to maintain those changes for a longer period of time. Without your mind on board, reengaging in old habits or letting old triggers pull you back into a cluttered state of living becomes a lot easier.

In order to effectively embrace the practice of changing your mindset, I highly recommend that you pick up a journal that you are going to use to help you address your mindset patterns. In this journal, refrain from having any particular rhyme or reason for how things are organized or what is inside of it. Instead, simply use it to write out your thoughts and get your inner feelings out on paper in any order that they feel like coming out in. That way, you can see exactly what it is that you are holding on to and how it is holding you back. I recommend using this book throughout the entire decluttering process, as it will give you a spot to write down why you are feeling so attached to certain things in your life and how you can release those attachments so that you can embrace a better life.

Identifying Your Core Values

Every single person on the planet has core values, whether they are consciously aware of these values or not. Your core values are things that you care about the most and that you will consistently value above anything else in your life. Your core values highlight what you stand for, what you care about, and why you behave the way that you do. When you are consciously aware of your core values, you can understand what drives you and motivates you and begin living in alignment with them so that you experience a consistent and deep sense of fulfillment. When you are not consciously aware of them, or if you are but you are failing to honor them, your core values become a source of pain because you find yourself living out of alignment with what matters to you. As a result, you begin to enforce bad habits and childish behavior as a way to cope and experience some form of relief from the pain of not honoring your values.

Discovering what your personal values are is imperative because it allows you to begin making conscious changes in your life that will support you in honoring these values. Although your values may seem mysterious and unknown in the present, it is actually not too hard to identify your core values and begin acting in alignment with them, so that you can continue experiencing fulfillment and joy in your life.

Before you begin discovering your core values, it is important that you take a few minutes to discard any values that you may be carrying from society or as a result of the beliefs that others have bestowed upon you. For example, if society tells you that you should value money but you find that money is not that important to you, do not feel obligated to hold financial wealth as one of your core values simply because society said so. Many people, particularly those who do not take the time to discover their core values, hold on to societal values and believe that they genuinely reflect their own personal values, too. If a value does not resonate with you, you are not obligated to maintain that value, even if it seems like you should because society told you that you must.

Once you have given yourself permission to discard the values of the society that do not resonate with you, you can start identifying your core values based on what does matter to you. The best way to do this is to begin journaling about what truly matters to you. If you are not yet sure, consider writing down all of the times when you feel your best in life. The moments that you feel motivated, inspired, and ready to jump into action are typically the same moments that you are living in alignment with your values. Pay attention to what common themes arise in these moments and use them as an opportunity to identify what matters the most to you. These will be your core values.

Overcoming Procrastination

One of the biggest reasons why people procrastinate in their lives is because they are unhappy with the lives that they are living and they use procrastination as a means to avoid doing the things that they don't want to do. While you cannot avoid doing things you do not want to do in certain cases, you can offset this reaction by increasing the number of positive things that you get to enjoy in your daily life. By creating a more harmonious balance between what you enjoy and what you have to get done, it becomes easier to do the things that you need to do because you are approaching your life from a more enjoyable and positive frame of mind.

In addition to balancing out your schedule to accommodate for more of what you enjoy and value, there are also some other ways that you can decrease your tendency to procrastinate and increase your ability to focus and get things done. Many of these practices are rooted in the mind and in learning how to motivate yourself so that you can stop being charmed by distractions are start taking productive actions towards succeeding in achieving your goals.

One great way that you can overcome procrastination is by setting a time restriction on how long you are allowed to put things off for and then actually adhering to that restriction. For example, say you have a tendency to get distracted anytime you are engaging in an activity that needs to get done. You might set a rule for yourself that you will give yourself the opportunity to spend 5 minutes being distracted before you get started, and then set a timer and fulfill those 5 minutes with distractions. This is an opportunity to get anything distracting out of the way so that you can clearly focus once you get to work. Then, if you notice that you tend to get distracted again at certain points into your work, you can schedule additional distraction breaks. For example, say around one hour into doing any task, you find yourself feeling distracted and struggling to stay focused. Rather than trying to push through the distraction and work with half of your focus, you can instead give yourself 5 minutes to be distracted and then return to focusing on your task at hand. By intentionally giving yourself permission to take 5 minutes here and there to indulge in your distractions, you ensure that you are not allowing them to take over and prevent you from getting started or completing your work.

Another thing that you can do is promise yourself a reward anytime you engage in a new task and fully completes it. Rewards show you that it is worthwhile to do things, even if they are things that you do not necessarily enjoy so that you can begin getting tasks done without such a struggle. Plus, they are a fun way to celebrate your success and your devotion to achieving your goals.

The final tip I want to give you is a mindset strategy that you can use called rephrasing. Rephrasing requires you to assess your inner dialogue around the subject and then consider how you can adjust it to keep yourself motivated and ready to achieve your tasks at hand. Often, when you are procrastinating, the inner dialogue that you are engaging in surrounding the task at hand is negative towards the task that needs to be achieved. By adjusting what you are saying to yourself, it becomes easier for you to find the energy and motivation to get up and get the task done. For example, instead of saying "I hate doing dishes. I don't want to do them. I'll do them later," you might say, "I love having a clean kitchen. I'm going to get it done so I can enjoy my clean space."

Releasing Negative Thought Patterns

Negative thought patterns are a form of mental clutter that does not serve you in any way, shape, or form. When you engage in negative thought patterns, you pressure yourself into feeling unconfident, incapable, or overwhelmed. Negative thought patterns are often at the foundation of every bad habit or experience we keep ourselves engaged in because we are able to justify them by lessening ourselves through our inner dialogue. Not only will they result in you lacking confidence and self-esteem, but they will also result in you feeling as though there is nothing positive or worthwhile for you to look forward to in your life. People who are constantly feeding into pessimistic thought patterns often find themselves feeling negative about everything that is going on in their lives. If you are someone who regularly complains, sees the bad in people or situations, or feels like there is nothing positive about yourself or the world around you, chances are that you are engaging in negative thought patterns.

A great way to begin decluttering your mind by releasing negative thought patterns is by engaging in activities such as cognitive behavioral therapy. This form of therapy does not require you to actually go and see a therapist so that you can check in on your negative thinking patterns. Instead, it allows you to identify what negative thoughts are leading to the negative emotions that you are experiencing and how you can intercept these thoughts so that you can adjust your emotions and, in turn, feel more confident and motivated.

In order to begin enforcing cognitive behavioral therapy in your own life, you can start keeping a journal where you track your thoughts and coinciding feelings on a regular basis. Each time you notice an intense or obvious negative emotion coming into your life, stop and consider what thoughts you are having and how they are contributing to that negative emotion. Then, once you have a general idea of what negative thought patterns you tend to follow, start consciously choosing new inner dialogues and activities to help you overcome these negative thoughts.

Increasing Your Mental Resiliency

Many people who are experiencing intense clutter in their lives and in their minds are also struggling with mental resiliency. Mental resiliency is the tool that you can use to help you focus your mind and bounce back from challenging or emotional situations with greater ease. You can build mental resiliency through practices like meditation, mindfulness, and rest. You can also build it by finding purpose in your life, as having a purpose is known to help people feel a greater sense of urgency when it comes to moving forward in their lives. People who lack purpose often find themselves feeling like there is no point in moving forward or accomplishing challenging tasks because there is no purpose behind the action itself. When you discover what your purpose is or create purpose and meaning in your day-to-day life, even as simple as cultivating your own contentment, you give yourself a reason to stay dedicated to more challenging practices.

You can also build your mental resiliency by choosing to put things into perspective and through realizing that not everything is as challenging as it may sound. When you see that all of your problems can be overcome and that they will not last forever, it becomes easier to prevent them from feeling all-consuming. This means that you no longer feel as though you simply cannot overcome challenges because they do not seem quite so large and daunting. When it comes to decluttering your mind, having resiliency is imperative as this is the key that is going to help you bounce back even after you have setbacks. Any time you find yourself struggling to maintain your clean space or feeling as though there is no reason for you to get up and make changes in your life, you can fall back on your mental resiliency as a tool to help you move forward and achieve success.

If you're enjoying this audiobook, I would love if you went to audible and just left a short review.

Chapter 3: Decluttering Your Home

The next step in decluttering your life is decluttering your home. They say that having a messy home reflects the fact that you likely also have a messy frame of mind, meaning that you likely hold onto a lot of stress and overwhelm. Now that you have made the conscious effort of moving past the mental clutter, you need to begin working on cleaning up your home, so that it can support you in having less stress to worry about. When you live in a clean and comfortable space, it becomes easier for you to rest, concentrate, and focus on achieving what you desire in your life because you are not wasting your attention on frustrations that arise in the midst of clutter.

In this chapter, we are going to look into how you can declutter your home and rejuvenate your living space. You are going to discover how you can eliminate clutter and create a cozier environment so that your home nurtures your ability to rest and relax, while also providing you a great launch pad for setting out to achieve all of your goals. You will never realize just how valuable your home is in regards to your mental wellness and your ability to live a successful life until you declutter it and let go of every block that has been holding you back.

How to Tackle the Decluttering of your Home

When you are decluttering your home, it is important that you do it on a step-by-step basis. If you are reading this book, the chances are that your home feels pretty overwhelming and frustrating to you right now. You may have already tried to declutter but it proved to be ineffective or you got overwhelmed and annoyed and were unable to finish the task. By working towards decluttering your home one step at a time, you can ensure that you are ready to face each task. You also prevent it from feeling daunting and overwhelming so it becomes easier for you to actually stay devoted to the task and get the job done.

I suggest following this chapter step-by-step in order so that you are able to accomplish the decluttering process in a way that will work alongside improving your inner contentment and wellbeing. By starting with the bedroom, you ensure that you are in a cozy and comfortable space each night when you go to sleep. Then, you can begin tackling each room based on how frequently they are used and how much they affect your sense of wellbeing.

Decluttering Your Bedroom

Your bedroom is where you lay your head to rest at night unless it is overwhelming and uncomfortable. Having a bedroom that is filled with clutter or that continually looks messy can be extremely stressful and overwhelming. Laying your head to sleep in a room that is cluttered can result in you not getting a sound sleep, or in you struggling to get any sleep at all. By tackling your bedroom first, you can ensure that you are able to start getting a sound sleep and improving your mental well-being right away using the art of decluttering as your secret weapon.

Below are six steps that you can use to declutter your room right now:

Eliminate Unwanted Clothes

Clothes tend to formulate the bulk of most messes in bedrooms. The best way for you to overcome this is to donate unwanted clothes so that you are not shoveling them out of the way every time you look for clothes that you actually want to wear.

Use Your Hamper

Instead of throwing your worn clothes on the floor, toss them into a hamper so that they are contained and cleaner looking. This also prevents you from having to determine what is clean and what isn't. Make sure that you get into the habit of putting clothes directly into your hamper so that you don't have to do it later.

Use Containers to Contain the Clutter

If you tend to store little things in your room such as jewelry, keys, or other little things, start using small containers to contain them. Bowls, trays, and small baskets or boxes are great tools for organizing smaller clutter that does not have a space to stay long-term.

Organize Your Closet

Your closet is an important area of your room to organize, too. Invest in shelves, shoe storage, and proper hangers and start making use of the space that you have in your closet. Get into the habit of hanging your clothes and returning your shoes to their spot so that they are always organized and out of the way.

Use Minimalistic Decorations

Make sure that the decorations you use in your bedroom are minimalistic and calm and relaxed in their design. Having anything too bold, bright, or overwhelming can keep your mind busy and prevent you from having a sound sleep each night. Think in terms of decorating with minimalistic paintings, candles, and soft fabrics.

Decluttering Your Kitchen

Your kitchen should be your next order of business. You use your kitchen on a daily basis, which means that it can quickly and easily become cluttered and messy consistently. In fact, you may feel like all you ever do is clean your kitchen when you are home because of the number of dishes, cookware, and utensils that you go through. Organizing your kitchen and decluttering it will help you eliminate this stress and keep your kitchen cleaner so that you do not feel like you are constantly battling a messy space.

Below are seven steps you can take to create a cleaner kitchen.

Eliminate the Excess Junk

Start by getting rid of all of the dishes, small appliances, and other odds and ends that you don't use anymore. Kitchen cabinets and drawers tend to be a place where junk goes to hide, so pulling everything out and eliminating unwanted space is a good place to start.

Take Advantage of Storage Space

As you begin putting your kitchen back together, be sure to take advantage of storage space when you are putting everything back. Do not be afraid to hang hooks so that you can make use of vertical storage, or add lazy Susan's into your cupboards for easier access.

Keep Your Counters Clear

Counters tend to accumulate a lot of mess and look disastrous on a consistent basis. Eliminate everything from your counters except for your coffee pot and your microwave. Make a rule that nothing gets stored on the counters anymore.

Use Storage Solutions for Cleaner Drawers and Cupboards

There are many incredible tools that you can buy to organize your drawers and cupboards. Get a matching storage set for all of your dry ingredients, a functional utensil tray for your utensils, and small baskets to organize other odds and ends into.

Build a Communications Center

One thing that tends to build up in the kitchen is the day-to-day tools like purses, keys, cell phone chargers, and other odds and ends. Creating a communications center to store all of these things makes it much easier for you to avoid having them scattered about on the counter. Outfit your space with a calendar, some hanging hooks, and a small drawer set if you can so that you have plenty of space to store things and keep them off of your counters.

Clean Out Underneath Your Sink

Whether you store cleaners, garbage, or both underneath your sink, this space can accumulate a lot of junk if you are not careful. Pull everything out, wipe it down, and only replace the things that you actually use or need. Toss the rest.

Clean Out Your Food Supply

The final thing you need to do when decluttering your kitchen is to clean out your food supply. Eliminate all of the food from your pantry, cupboards, fridge, and freezer that you are not eating. Even if it has not yet expired, do not keep it if you do not want it. It only takes up space and makes you feel guilty that you wasted your money on it.

Decluttering Your Living Room

The next space you need to declutter is your living room. The living room tends to be another area that accumulates a lot of day-to-day essentials and random clutter since it tends to be where most people spend their time when they are home, aside from the kitchen. Decluttering your living room requires you to ensure that you are staying consistent when it comes to keeping everything out of the living room long-term.

Below are four strategies that you can use to declutter your living room.

Return Everything to Where It Belongs

Begin by taking a moment to remove everything out of the living room that does not belong there. Return clothes back to where they belong, put their shoes in their space, bring dishes back into the kitchen, and put the toys back in your kids' rooms.

Use A Declutter Basket

Decluttering baskets are great in living rooms because they make returning stuff to other parts of the house easier. Keep a basket in your living room and each time you find something in the living room that doesn't belong, toss it in the basket. At the end of each day, put everything back where it belongs.

Organize Your Media Cabinet

Media cabinets can become messy with cords, games, movies, and other gadgets. Take some time to organize your media cabinet by organizing your cords, stacking games and DVDs nicely, and putting other odds and ends into small storage containers that you can store in the media cabinet. That way, everything looks neat and it is also easier to find.

Minimize Your Decorations

While your living room offers far more flexibility when it comes to decorations, you should still be cautious about what you add to this space. Think about decorating with quality, not quantity, so that you do not have so many things to dust, move around, or organize when it comes time to clean up.

Decluttering Your Bathrooms

While your bathrooms are used multiple times a day, they are not necessarily known for being the worst when it comes to clutter. However, because the type of clutter that accumulates is often filled with various liquids and products, they can spill over and create an unsightly mess. For that reason, you need to have a proper decluttering regimen in place that minimizes the amount of stuff you keep and keeps it organized so that you are not finding your bathroom looking overwhelmed with a mess.

Below are three strategies that you can use to declutter your bathroom.

Eliminated Unwanted Products

Products that are typically stored in the bathroom can be expensive, which is why most people feel guilty about throwing away the things that they are not using. However, this can result in you having a tremendous amount of clutter built up in a small space. Start your decluttering process by throwing away every single product that you have not used in more than one month.

Clean Absolutely Everything Off

Now that you have eliminated unwanted products, you need to clean everything off. Wipe dirt and grime off of product bottles, wipe out cupboards and drawers, and wipe down your sink and mirror while you are at it. Then, put everything away neatly in the newly cleaned space.

Use Effective Storage Solutions

When it comes to putting things back, make sure that you are doing so in a way that makes sense. Consider investing in small baskets to organize products into, use a shower caddy to store your shower products in, and get a toilet roll holder to hold extra toilet paper rolls in the bathroom. You may also consider using a small shelf under your sink so that you have more storage space for products and beauty tools.

Decluttering Storage

There are likely many other storage areas in your home that have not yet been discussed in this chapter. While these are not used as frequently or intensely as other areas in your home, they can become extremely messy and overwhelming if you are not careful. Coat closets, storage closets, garages, storage rooms, and other spaces can become messy if you are not maintaining them well.

Below are three strategies that you can use to declutter your storage spaces.

Commit To Going through Everything

It may be an overwhelming task, but you should commit to going through everything that you have in storage. If you have not done this in a while, you may be surprised to find that you are holding onto a lot of junk that you do not need anymore. Set aside a day, or a few days, where you are going to go through your storage spaces and organize everything. In that time, eliminate everything you do not want, pull out things you want to start using regularly, and organize the things that you want to put back into storage into logical categories.

Use Labeled Bins

When you have determined what is ready to go back into storage, you can go ahead and purchase some labeled bins to store everything in. Even if you already have some bins, you might consider purchasing all new ones that are similar in size, shape, and color. That way, when everything is put away, it looks visually appealing, which will help it produce less stress each time you look at it. Label bins clearly so that you know exactly what has been stored inside of them.

Keep the Space Clean

Even though it may seem pointless, commit to regularly vacuuming and dusting your storage spaces. Doing so will ensure that you are not accumulating large amounts of dust and dirt in these areas, which will help them look and feel more organized each time you go into them.

Chapter 4: Decluttering Your Finances

The next task you are going to want to tackle when it comes to decluttering your life is decluttering your finances. Finances tend to become overwhelmed with excess burdens, money leaking out in places that it shouldn't be, and chaos or confusion being thrown into the pile. If you have no idea where your money is going, find yourself paying for bills that you don't even recognize, or have services that are going unused, it is time for you to do a financial decluttering. That way, you can ensure that you are not wasting your money, that you have more to save, and that when you spend it, you actually spend it on things that are meaningful and purposeful.

In this chapter, we are going to explore four critical areas that you need to consider in your finances when it comes to building budgets. These areas are going to support you in making sure that your finances are being properly managed. In doing so, not only will you bring less chaos and confusion around your finances, but you will also bring more peace and relaxation into your life. Finances tend to be one of the biggest areas where chaos and overwhelming stresses seep into people's lives, especially if they find themselves coming under financial strain on a regular basis. Organizing your finances will ensure that you are not wasting money or stressing unnecessarily over things that do not matter.

Mastering the Art of Budgeting

Budgeting is a valuable tool that can help ensure that you are not wasting finances on unnecessary expenses or overspending in areas of your life where you should be saving more. Creating a functional budget for you is extremely simple.All it requires of you is for you to take an honest account of what you are earning and what you are spending on a monthly basis. This way, you can identify where your money needs to be spent and how you can be spending it wisely on a weekly and monthly basis.

The best way to start your budget is to write down how much money you bring in each month. Write this down on a piece of paper at the top of the page. Then, underneath that number, write down every mandatory expense that you need to be spending on a monthly basis. This includes your car payments, gas bills, rent, utilities, groceries, and other mandatory expenses that you need to be paying in order to maintain your basic needs. Underneath those, include the additional expenses that you tend to find yourself using on a consistent basis. This typically includes money spent on clothes, entertainment, and other more frivolous purchases that you may enjoy making on a monthly basis. This is going to give you an idea of where your money is being spent and how so that you have a clearer understanding as to how your money is being used.

As you go through your budget, take account of any subscriptions or other monthly expenses that you are incurring that are not necessary or that you do not actually use. For example, if you have a Netflix subscription or some magazine subscriptions but you find that you are never actively using them, you can cancel these and save yourself the monthly expense. That way, you are not wasting money on things that do not matter to you.

The last thing that you need to do is consider how much you want to be saving on a monthly basis. The best way to do this is to create savings goals for you. You should have short-term savings goals that you want to see met in the next 6-12 months, as well as long-term savings goals that you have for five, ten, fifteen, and twenty years from now. If you are significantly younger and you have many more years to go before you reach a retirement age, set your retirement savings goal as well. With these goals in mind, calculate how much you need to be saving on a monthly basis in order to meet these goals. Then, go ahead and factor that in as a necessary expense on your monthly bills. This savings value should come before any of your luxury expenses such as entertainment, as this money will be used to help you sustain a higher quality of living in the long run.

Releasing Financial Burdens You Don't Need

It is important that you really crack down on financial burdens that you are incurring that you do not need. Financial burdens can be anything from subscriptions that you are not using to debt that you are not paying off quick enough. Getting clear on what funds are being wasted on expenses such as this will help you determine whether or not your budget is working in your favor. Eliminating unnecessary expenses and debt will ensure that you are not spending money that you do not need to be spending on a monthly basis.

If you are attempting to cut down on your debt, I recommend putting this above anything else for a while. Get strict on the amount of money that you are willing to spend on new purchases until your debt is completely cleared so that you are no longer wasting money on unnecessary expenses such as high-interest fees and annual charges. That way, your debt is cleared faster and you actually end up saving significantly more every single month.

Some people accumulate a high amount of debt which can make looking at your debt and getting serious on how much you owe scary or even nauseating. Debt can be uncomfortable and frustrating if you are not taking control over it, which makes it understandable as to why so many people attempt to avoid the reality of their debt. Even so, if you want to have a cleaner financial life, you need to eliminate unnecessary debt from your life. The best way to do this is to write down exactly how much you owe and create a plan for how you are going to pay it off. Then, pay into that debt every single month until it is completely eliminated. Avoid spending money, in any way, that could further increase your debt until you have completely paid it off and you are confident that you can manage your debt more wisely in the future.

Having Weekly Spending Limits

Most people want to enjoy the money that they earn so they find themselves regularly indulging in spending money on things like coffees, clothes, convenience services, and other unnecessary expenses. When it is not managed effectively, these types of expenses can quickly rack up and result in you having no money left. In order to avoid spending every last dollar you have on unnecessary expenses, start setting weekly spending limits for yourself. Give yourself a fixed amount that you are allowed to spend on enjoyable things on a weekly basis and be strict in adhering to that amount. That way, you are no longer spending money faster than you are making it and committing to things like paying off debt and saving funds becomes a lot easier for you.

Your weekly spending limit should be reasonable, and it should always come last after your necessary expenses, your debt repayment, and your savings funds. Choose a limit that is going to give you a bit of cash to have fun with, without taking away from other expenses that are more important. Once you pay off your debt or begin earning a higher income, you can increase the number of funds that you have to spend on a weekly basis. Until then, be strict with yourself and your money and commit to paying off your debt now, so that you can pay for your fun and entertainment with ease and less stress later.

Taking the Occasional Cash Freeze Break

If you are someone who tends to spend money without thinking about it, or who relies on things like retail therapy to help you get through challenging times, it is time for you to engage in what is known as a "cash freeze breaks." These breaks are things that some people engage in from time to time to encourage themselves to find other ways to deal with a bad mood or boredom. The rules are simple: for a fixed amount of time, usually a week, you will not spend any money unless it is going towards mandatory bills and expenses. No spending money on entertainment, additional food items, or anything else that would be considered not absolutely necessary in the way of having your basic needs met.

Doing spending freezes allows you to become creative in finding other ways to deal with the emotions or feelings that typically lead to you spending money unnecessarily. Not only does this encourage you to choose healthier coping methods, but it also prevents you from cluttering your house up with unnecessary impulse buys again. That way, you are not bringing home things that will only be donated or thrown out at a later date. Engaging in a spending freeze any time you find your impulsive purchases becoming excessive will ensure that you are staying on top of your spending habits and maintaining a healthy, clutter-free relationship with your finances.

Chapter 5: Decluttering Your Relationships

Relationships have the ability to become toxic and overwhelming in your life. If you are engaging in relationships that do not bring you joy, make you feel inspired or enriched, or help you to live a better life, chances are that you are carrying clutter in your relationships. As adults, we tend to not have much time to allot to things like friends and hobbies because we have so many demands on our time, such as work, family, and other errands that need to be run in order to maintain our daily lives. For that reason, it is imperative that you stay strict on who enters your life and how they contribute to the quality of your life. Cluttering up what little time you have to invest in friends and fun with people who are leaving you feeling frustrated, uncomfortable, or pained are only going to result in you feeling an increase in stress and overwhelm. As a result, you are going to experience a lower quality of life and a reduced desire to contribute to your experiencing more joy and positivity.

In this chapter, we are going to look at ways that you can identify clutter in your social circle and eliminate the people who are not contributing to the wellbeing of your general life. By identifying toxic people or meaningless relationships and eliminating them, you give yourself more time to devote to the relationships that actually mean something to you in your life. That way, you are spending what time you do have on relationships that are enriching and that lift you up and help you feel inspired to continue doing better in your everyday life.

Identifying Clutter in Your Social Circle

The first thing that you need to do when it comes to decluttering your social circle is to identify where the clutter actually exists. They say that you are the sum of the five people that you spend most of your time with. Looking at the five people that you spend your time with helps you to determine who they are and, as a result, who you are. If these people are inspiring, uplifting, positive, and motivated, then chances are you are surrounding yourself with great people who are helping lift you up and motivate you in your own life. However, if you look around and see people who lack motivation, who regularly make excuses for themselves, and who struggle to make positive changes in their lives, then chances are that you are struggling with all of the same things. For that reason, you need to get clear on where the clutter lies and how you can clean it up to avoid being dragged down anymore.

In some relationships, the clutter is not necessarily the person themselves, but instead, in the way that your relationship manifests. For example, maybe you have a relationship with a really positive and inspiring person but the only time you spend together is spent doing meaningless tasks or things that you do not enjoy. In that case, the relationship may be cluttered with you not being willing to speak up for yourself or what you enjoy, or with the fact that even though you are both great people, you simply do not connect in an effective manner.

Identifying clutter in your relationships and in your social circle, in general, helps you begin making effective action plans so that you can determine what needs to be done, allowing you to experience less clutter in your relationships. Whether that is adjusting how you spend your time together, speaking up for yourself more and building more of a quality connection, or moving on and finding a friend who is better suited for you, that will ultimately be up to you.

Some people are unwilling to leave everyone behind, particularly if the relationship in question is one that is shared between someone you care about but do not necessarily get along with very well, such as a parent or a sibling. In some cases, this may even be a lifelong best friend whom you do not want to cut out of your life but whom you struggle to experience positive interactions with anymore. In these scenarios, there are many different solutions that you can come up with to avoid having to actually remove said person from your life. For example, spending less time with them, or being more selective about what you engage in together so that there is less of an opportunity for the negative or toxic traits to arise. You may also consider chatting with this person and encouraging them to engage in some healthy self-reflection so that they can see where their own negativity may be bringing them down. If you do choose to engage in a conversation like this, make sure that you do it gently and mindfully, so that it doesn't sound like you are attacking or belittling the other person. That way, it is more likely to be a constructive conversation than one that results in them feeling angry and an argument transpiring in your relationship, which can lead to further stress.

Removing Toxic Relationships from Your Life

When it comes to dealing with toxic relationships in your life, finding the right way to navigate the ending of these relationships can be challenging. You may struggle to understand how you can approach the situation in a way that is going to allow you to confidently and successfully end the relationship without causing too many hurt feelings. Unfortunately, hurt feelings are almost completely unavoidable when it comes to navigating the ending of challenging relationships in your life, so ending the relationship in a way where absolutely no feelings are hurt is going to be tough. For that reason, it is important that you understand that hurt feelings are going to be a part of the equation so that you can manage it in a way that minimizes the number of feelings that are being hurt.

With that in mind, there are a few things that you can do to end toxic relationships in a healthy and positive manner so that you can avoid doing extra or unnecessary damage in the process. The following three steps will help you successfully end unhealthy and toxic relationships in the most effective and polite manner possible.

Be Completely Honest From the Start

If you have already tried using other methods to improve the relationship that you share with a toxic person and they do not seem to be working for you, then it is time for you to move on to a new plan. That plan should be for you to completely end the relationship so that you can avoid having to suffer from the other person's toxic behaviors and attitude any longer. In order for you to successfully end a toxic relationship, you need to be completely honest right from the start. Being honest will prevent you from creating further hurt feelings by lying or trying to protect their feelings, which are already being hurt because you are ending your relationship with them. The best way to lessen the blow is to be honest and kind with everything you say.

Avoid Playing the Blame Game

When you end a relationship that is toxic, avoid playing the blame game and making it sound like you are attacking the other person or victimizing yourself from the relationship. Even though they have been toxic, recognize that there is a chance that you have been contributing to the toxic behavior in some way. In realizing this, avoid bringing up any arguments that may make it sound like you are ending the relationship because the other person is in any way bad. Even if they have done bad things, do not blame them or become harsh or attacking towards them in pointing out the truth. Always be polite and use "I" statements so that you own your feelings and your responsibility in the situation. That way, you are not hurting their feelings and you are not creating the opportunity for them to victimize themselves and potentially use that against you in the future.

End the Relationship Completely

If you have arrived at the point where you feel as though you need to end a relationship with someone, make sure that you completely end the relationship that you share with this person. Trying to hold onto the relationship or create hope when there is no hope to be had will only result in you feeling prolonged effects of their toxic behaviors. Cut off the relationship completely by eliminating all means of communication and contact with this person. Do not call them or text them any longer, do not keep them on your social media accounts, and do not spend time with them if you come across them in public. Instead, nod or say a polite hello and move along. Attempting to rekindle toxic relationships is only going to result in you exposing yourself to the toxic behavior once again. As hard as it is, you need to completely end the relationship and keep it that way so that you are not bringing the clutter of toxicity back into your life over and over again.

Cleaning Up Your Social Media

Another part of your social life that you need to focus on cleaning up is your social media. Social media has a tendency to be a place where you accumulate a lot of friends and followers who hang around and rarely interact with you or maintain a relationship with you. Frequently, these relationships are held onto out of obligation or for no real reason at all, such as when you add people you went to high school with and then never saw – or talked to – again. Although it may seem nice and comforting to have these people around, the reality is that you are just holding onto clutter for no real reason. Instead of holding onto friends and followers on Facebook, Instagram, Pinterest, and other accounts that you spend time on, regularly purge your friends' lists and eliminate anyone whom you do not genuinely enjoy interacting with.

You should also set aside time to do this with your email. Our inboxes can quickly become flooded with so many different newsletters, spam messages, and other strange messages that come in from seemingly nowhere. These messages can be overwhelming and can waste your time, as you have to go through and delete them every single time that they come in. Instead of accumulating junk mail in your inbox, spend time unsubscribing from every email list that you do not actually care about receiving. Furthermore, avoid signing up for newsletters in the future unless you actually stand to gain something meaningful or valuable out of them. That way, you do not have to waste your time continually purging your email account over and over again.

Lastly, go on your phone and sort through all of your contacts and text messages. Go ahead and eliminate any contacts that you no longer require or use, and erase any text messages that are not important. Though this may seem unnecessary or pointless to you, it can actually do a world of wonders on your mindset. Not having to scroll past the names of people you no longer talk to means no longer having an uncomfortable feeling of being obligated to reach out to them and see how they are doing, despite it being totally unnecessary and even pointless. Instead, simply eliminate these people from your contact list, so that you do not have to worry about them any longer.

Being More Present atthe Moment

Now that you have eliminated everything that has been creating stress and overwhelming feelings in your life in regards to your relationships and social circle, you can start focusing on taking advantage of your new clutter-free space! Spend time focusing on learning how to become present at the moment so that you can stay present and genuinely enjoy the time that you share with the people who matter to you. By staying present and enjoying each moment for what it is, you maximize the quality of your friendships and they become even more rewarding and enjoyable. As a result, you are able to feel more enriched by your relationships and make sure that *you* aren't the one bringing clutter into the relationship and making it toxic.

Being present is an opportunity for you to unite your uncluttered mindset with your uncluttered relationships and experience more joy and positivity in your life. As you begin to embrace presence in your relationships, seek to begin working on new ways to enjoy these relationships even further. Take up hobbies with your friends, enjoy trying new things, fully engage in the experiences that you share, and make each moment meaningful. When you share time together, put your phone down, and avoid stressing or worrying about things that truly do not matter. Do not engage in gossip, complain about everything under the sun, and bring an overall negative energy to the relationship. Instead, work towards creating a positive, enjoyable, and real relationship with the people that you care about.

If presence is particularly challenging for you because your mind still tends to be overwhelmed by clutter, start using some presence practices to help you bring your focus back into the moment. You can do this by using your negative thought pattern reprogramming practices from chapter 2 actively during the time you share with friends, engaging in self-awareness, and practicing self-reflection. By truly paying attention to how you spend your time and where you place your focus, you can ensure that you are only spending your time on things that matter in your life.

Making Time for the Ones You Love

The last thing you need to do when it comes to decluttering your relationships is decluttering the excuses that prevent you from not investing more time and energy into your relationships. Now that your house is clean, your finances are cleared, and you are no longer being overwhelmed by negative thoughts, you can start enjoying more time with the people you love. You can do this by making sure that you actually set aside time for you to spend with your loved ones so that you are seeing them and investing in your relationship with them on a regular basis.

The best way to make sure that you are consistently setting aside time for your loved ones is to schedule aside a bit of time each week to invest in your relationships. You can spend this time physically visiting with them, or talking with them on the phone if visiting is not an option. You can also ensure that every now and again, you send them a text message or an email letting them know that you are thinking about them and taking a moment to catch up with them and see how they are doing. By regularly investing your time and energy into your meaningful relationships, you ensure that you are keeping your relationships fulfilled and that they thrive. Through actions like this, your loved ones know that you care about them and feel as though they are genuinely meaningful to you. As a result, your relationships grow even stronger and the rewards that you reap from them are increased as you derive even more joy and meaning from your relationships.

If you're enjoying this book, I would appreciate it if you went to the place of purchase and left a short positive review. Thank you

Chapter 6: Healthy Habits for Decluttering

You have now successfully invested in decluttering all of the most important aspects of your life. From your mindset to your home, you have discovered everything you need to know in order to fully declutter your life and start experiencing greater joy and rewards from it. Of course, there are always ways for you to improve your ability to declutter and stay clutter-free and stress-free, so in this chapter, I am going to show you how you can engage in healthy habits for decluttering your life even further. You should implement these habits into your life to ensure that you are experiencing the most fulfillment and joy that you possibly can from your life.

Take Things Slowly, There Is No Rush

When it comes to accomplishing something like decluttering your life, most of us have a tendency to get a massive wave of motivation that results in us wanting to get everything done all at once. While this motivation can be powerful, it can also be overwhelming and can lead to you struggling to get anything done. Instead of trying to get it all done at once, give yourself permission to take your time and work through the decluttering process at a rate that is more reasonable for you. This does not mean that you should infuse the process with more procrastination, but don't be afraid to span your decluttering out over a few weeks or a month so that you have plenty of time to get everything done without enduring quite so much stress.

One of the biggest reasons why people become so overwhelmed by decluttering is that they are trying to get everything done immediately. You need to realize that it has taken you a long time to accumulate all of the clutter that you currently have, so it will also take you some time to eliminate it. Although the elimination process will be quicker because it is more intentional and focused, it will still take time. Give yourself the time you need to successfully get through all of the tasks so that you do not experience so much overwhelm and stress along the way.

Be Practical about What You Can Achieve

When it comes to eliminating clutter from your life, you also need to be practical. If you are someone who has been known for hoarding a lot more than you need, then completely eliminating everything the first time around may be excessive and extremely overwhelming for you to embrace. You may need to take things slowly and declutter in phases, by eliminating a few things at a time until you reach a state that feels more comfortable to you. That way, you are not shocking yourself by getting rid of everything and feeling a sense of fear and discomfort as you attempt to get used to not having any of your previous comforts around.

This is especially true when it comes to dealing with finances. When you work towards decluttering your finances, you may find yourself becoming intensely strict on your budget and attempting to cut down on absolutely everything. While this is not harmful in most cases, in some cases, it can become overwhelming or overly restricting if you find yourself trying to achieve too much at once. Instead of trying to get everything done in one go, be practical about what you can accomplish and build from there.

Do Not Be Afraid To Ask For Support

When you are decluttering, it is not unreasonable to ask people to support you and help you successfully get through the process of decluttering. This is even more important if you are someone who struggles with mobility issues or who has some form of physical limitation that prevents you from being able to do too much at once. Instead of attempting to pressure yourself into doing everything alone, be willing to ask for the support of those around you. See who is willing to help you and then do not be afraid to call on them when you need it.

Friends and family can be supportive by helping you pack boxes, organize your belongings back into your new containers, or transport unwanted goods to donation drop-offs. If they are willing to, asking them to help you can be a powerful way to get through everything without feeling quite as stressed out. When you ask, make sure that you truly give yourself permission to receive their help along the way. If you are feeling ashamed about your space or about the mess that you have accumulated, realize that your friends and family have likely already seen it or are experiencing similar issues in their own lives. Most people are not afraid of clutter, nor will they think any less of you if they see that you have clutter in your home. If they do, they are likely individuals that fall into the "toxic" or "clutter" category in your relationships, so letting go of them is not unreasonable.

Take Before and After Photographs

A great way to motivate yourself to keep going and to celebrate how far you have come is to take before and after photographs of your space (to positively inspire you by) as so positive and inspired by the work that you have done, so that it will feel easier for you to move through the cleaning process. Snapping before photographs of rooms, drawers, and messy corners and then snapping after pictures is a great way for you to really see how much work you have done and how much better it looks. When you look at these pictures, you will feel to understand the meaning behind it all and celebrate yourself for your success.

You can also use these photographs to motivate you anytime you see your house becoming messy or cluttered again. Simply sneaking a peek at your before picture and remembering how much work it took for you to get from there to your newer clutter-free space may be plenty to help encourage you to stay on track with your wiser spending habits, your cleaning habits, and your intentional decluttering habits.

Be Compassionate With Yourself

Many people find that decluttering can be incredibility emotional, and they are rarely ready to endure the emotions that come with decluttering. When you eliminate clutter from your house, you may feel all sorts of different feelings. From embarrassment and shame around how far you have let it get to, to feelings of anger and resentment for the memories that are being triggered by your clutter, you may experience many emotions along the way. Being patient and compassionate with yourself when you are decluttering is essentialso that you do not add any additional unnecessary stress to the mix by belittling or bullying yourself in the process.

Realize that your accumulation of clutter was not intentional, nor was it ever meant to cause stress or frustration in your current life. It is likely that you accumulated this clutter by accident, or as a way to cope with challenging emotions that you were not ready to face in the past. If you find that the experience becomes too emotional, use this as an opportunity to lean on your support system, or even begin talking to a therapist for a while. To have someone to talk to about the emotions that are being brought up, especially if they are relating to grief or anger, can be a great way to work through unresolved issues that you may have been holding onto alongside your clutter. Doing this will ensure that you are staying healthy and mentally supported along the way so that you are not feeling so burdened by everything that you are facing.

Make It a Fun Experience

Just because you are cleaning does not mean that you cannot have fun! If you find decluttering to be boring and laborious, consider including activities to make it a more fun experience. Turn on some music and dance along to it, or see how much you can get done during a single song. Give yourself rewards along the way, spend time playing with the gadgets that you have uncovered and seeing if they will have any purpose in your life, and genuinely find joy in the process. You might even make it a game to see how much you can donate. Maybe, if the donation process is more challenging for you, you might consider making up pretend scenarios in your head of the future people who are going to use your items and get joy from them. This will help it not only become more of a game but will also help you see the benefit and value behind what you are doing. The more fun you make it; the easier it will be for you to continue on with the process.

Use a Quarantine Practice If You Need To

If you are attempting to decide what you want to get rid of but you are unsure about whether or not you are ready to get rid of some things, consider using the quarantine method to help you officially make up your mind. This is going to support you in deciding what you truly do want to get rid of, and what you may prefer to keep instead. The quarantine method essentially requires you to have a box or two where you will place items that you are unsure about. Everything you are questioning will go into this box and then be left for a month, maybe two at the very most. Anything that does not get retrieved from the box in that time should be donated so that you are not holding onto anything that you are not going to use.

The quarantine method is not only great for helping you eliminate unwanted things, but also for helping you avoid purchasing new things that you may not actually need or even want. In order to use it to help you shop more wisely, simply consider what landed in the box last time and how you had believed it would be more valuable to you than it was. Then, consider if what you are looking to purchase will actually be valuable to you or if you are going to end up putting it in the quarantine box or donation bin in the near future. If you find that it is likely going to end up there, you can simply save yourself the expense and avoid wasting your money by not purchasing the item at all. That way, you do not waste money on unnecessary things and you do not need to eliminate clutter from your home so frequently anymore.

Look atthe Positive Side of Things

As you go about the process of decluttering, it can be easy to see it as a hassle or feel guilty or upset about the things that you are eliminating. You may attempt to justify them or barter with yourself to talk yourself into keeping them because you feel so guilty about purchasing something that ended up being wasteful in the end. This type of mentality can be further amplified by a negative mindset along the way. Taking your time to focus on your mindset and using this as an opportunity to really consider your thought processes is a great opportunity for you to ensure that you are looking on the bright side of things and making the most out of the situation.

Instead of seeing the experience as being negative or embarrassing, embrace it as a learning experience and a moment of growth. Choose to celebrate yourself for the massive changes that you are making towards experiencing a more positive future, and really embody those feelings of celebration and joy. The more you look at the bright side of things and see all of the positives that you are gaining from your decluttering, the better the process will feel in general.

Begin Building More Positivity into Your Life

As you move through the process of decluttering your life, do not wait to begin building more positive practices into it. There is no reason for you to put off your new positive experiences until you reach a certain point of your decluttering process or until you have fully completed it. In fact, that is actually not advisable as making yourself wait can only make the process of decluttering even harder. When you make yourself wait unnecessarily, you prevent yourself from seeing the value of the experience and you end up feeling as though it is pointless since you are not gaining any rewards from your efforts. Instead, start building new positive experiences into your life right away. As you declutter your mind, start infusing your life with a more positive practice that you genuinely enjoy, such as singing or laughing more. As you declutter your home, invest in doing more of what you enjoy since you no longer have to stress over the cleaning that needs to be done. As you declutter your relationships and finances, start going out more and doing more positive things (within your means) with the people whom you care about.

The sooner you begin infusing your life with the positive rewards of your practice, the sooner you will be able to genuinely enjoy your life. You will also start finding that the rewards of your decluttering practice are so great that it makes it far more meaningful and worthwhile in the long run. Giving yourself a greater opportunity to focus on the positive aspects of your life will keep you motivated and moving forward, making it easier for you to continue living a continually happier life.

Conclusion

Congratulations on completing *Declutter!*

I hope that this book was effective in helping you understand the power of decluttering, the best methods for doing so, and healthy habits you can pick up along the way to ensure that you are maintaining a healthy sense of wellbeing as you go. Decluttering can be one of the most rewarding experiences there is, but it can also be one of the most trying experiences. As you go through a lifetime of belongings, memories, and emotions, it can be exhausting and overwhelming to face everything. Remember, you do not have to rush the experience and you are always able to ask for help and rely on support to get you through the process. Be reasonable with your expectations and work at a pace that serves you, not one that leads to you experiencing feelings of shock and overwhelm.

As you move forward after the process of decluttering, I strongly encourage you to continue practicing every single step in this book along the way. Just because you have successfully decluttered does not mean that the clutter cannot sneak back in through unexpected means. By paying close attention to your habits and keeping an eye on your life and home, you can ensure that clutter has nowhere to accumulate and that it does not take over again. That way, you can maintain the positive and happy benefits of the decluttering process and avoid reverting back into the stress and chaos of having clutter in your life.

Make sure that as you go, you stay open to learning and you continue to practice compassion and empathy towards yourself. It is not uncommon for people who are new to living a decluttered, minimalistic lifestyle to find themselves reverting back into old habits of accumulating clutter and letting it pile up. Simply notice any time you see this happening and take the necessary action to create a solution and eliminate the clutter once again. As you continue reinforcing your new habits and practices, you will find that maintaining a clean and clutter-free life will become significantly easier for you.

Lastly, I hope that you find many great joys and blessings in your new clutter-free life! Thank you so much for reading this book.

If you've enjoyed this book, I would appreciate it if you went to the place of purchase and left a short positive review. Thank you

CODEPENDENCY

No more - The codependent recovery guide to cure wounded souls

Chris S Jennings

TABLE OF CONTENTS

CODEPENDENCY

INTRODUCTION **69**

CHAPTER 1: UNDERSTANDING CODEPENDENCY **71**

- What is Codependency? 71
- Characteristics of Codependency 74

CHAPTER 2: TYPES OF CODEPENDENT PERSONALITIES AND BEHAVIOR **79**

- The Martyr 79
- The Savior 80
- The Coach 80
- The Enabler 81
- Behaviors 82
  - *Controlling* 82
  - *Enabling* 84
  - *People-pleasing* 86
  - *Self-denigrating* 87
  - *Overreacting* 88

CHAPTER 3: TRAUMA, HEALING, AND FORGIVENESS **91**

- What causes codependency to develop in the first place? 91
- Self-awareness and Self-acceptance 94
- Paths to Recovery 96

CHAPTER 4: BEGINNING TO HEAL **101**

- Recognizing Unhealthy Behavior Patterns 101
- Developing Mindfulness 103
- Learning to Love Yourself 108
- Accepting Your Partner 110

CHAPTER 5: CHANGING CODEPENDENT RELATIONSHIPS **115**

- Developing Empathic Communication 116
- Nurturing Mutual Respect 119
- Establishing Trust 121

CHAPTER 6: BREAKING THE CYCLE OF CODEPENDENCY **125**

- What does a healthy relationship look like? 126

Maintaining a Mindful Relationship Dynamic 128
Knowing When to Walk Away 129
Living the Life You Want to Live 132

CONCLUSION **135**

Introduction

The term "codependency" describes a pattern of dysfunctional behavior and thought which some estimates indicate affects as many as ninety percent of people in the United States. Like many such disorders, it exists on a spectrum, ranging from mild to severe, and depending on the degree to which it impacts a given individual or individuals in a relationship can lead to more dire consequences than many people may realize. People who are codependent frequently suffer from depression, anxiety, and emotional instability brought on by dealing with perpetual chaos in their lives, and they may subsequently struggle with drug addiction, alcoholism, ulcers, high blood pressure, headaches, and heart disease as a result of the constant stress under which they must operate. In short, the ability of people facing these issues to function effectively, to live fulfilling lives, to realize their full potential, and to simply experience happiness and contentment can become impossible or at least seriously compromised.

The good news is that codependency is not necessarily a lifelong condition - it can be overcome. Understanding and recognizing unhealthy behavior is the vital first step to abate it and avoid the myriad mental and physical health problems that may otherwise be incurred. Once the problem is identified, it is possible to learn new methods of coping, ways to gain self-awareness and change your perspective of yourself, improve your relationships with other people, and allow you to welcome the happiness and contentment we all want but which so often eludes us. If you fear you may be codependent, you can change your life for the better.

The following chapters will discuss what codependency is, what it looks like, and how to identify it. Then, we'll look into ways to break the cycle of codependency and heal to reach a better, healthier, and more fulfilling relationship. By the end of this book, you will be able to put aside codependent behaviors and feel better about yourself and your relationships.

There are plenty of books on this subject on the market, so thanks again for choosing this one! Every effort was made to ensure it is full of as much useful information as possible. Please enjoy!

Chapter 1: Understanding Codependency

"There are almost as many definitions of codependency as there are experiences that represent it."

— *Melody Beattie, Author of 'Codependent No More: How to Stop Controlling Others and Start Caring for Yourself'*

What is Codependency?

The concept of codependency first originated to describe patterns of behavior common specifically to people in relationships with alcoholics or drug addicts. These people exhibit a compulsive tendency to over-compensate and make excuses for the behavior of the addicted person, thus enabling the addict to continue in their own irresponsible and unhealthy way of being. The codependent person then becomes "addicted" to helping the other person and to the relationship, depending on it to meet nearly all of his or her emotional and self-esteem needs. It is a static symbiosis in which both partners are trapped and neither partner can change or grow. Though the term has been in use as described since the middle of the 20th century, subsequent research has revealed that the characteristics of codependency are not found solely amongst the spouses and family members of the people suffering addiction but are much more prevalent in the general population than anyone previously considered. It was discovered that if you were raised in a dysfunctional family or had a parent who was chronically mentally or physically ill, you could also be codependent.

In essence, codependency is characterized by a dysfunctional, one-sided relationship. A dysfunctional relationship is one in which the matching of the personalities of both partners results in the opposite of appropriate relationship function. Instead of fostering communication and offering nurture and emotional support, those engaged in a relationship which is dysfunctional - or "toxic" - become diminished, defeated, and self-destructive. A one-sided relationship is one in which partners consistently give to the relationship or the other person more than they receive in return or more than they allow themselves to have. In relationships with codependency - which may exist between parents and children, brothers and sisters, friends, co-workers, spouses or romantic partners - this unhealthy interaction results in a toxic entanglement which is deeply emotionally, psychologically, and potentially physically damaging to all involved.

People in healthy relationships are able to depend on each other. That mutual dependence makes both people feel safe and secure, and that sense of security strengthens the bond between them while allowing them to still maintain their individuality and independence. In a codependent relationship, two people effectively surrender their independence and develop an unhealthy enmeshment that doesn't allow either person to grow. This pattern of thought, feeling, and behavior is a denial of the self and can result in self-loathing, which the codependent relationship partner then acts out through self-destructive or unduly self-sacrificial behavior. Codependents lose themselves in the relationship and in the life of the other person and come to depend entirely on what approval they receive from their partner for their very identity. Their meaning and purpose are derived from striving to fulfill the needs of others at the expense of their own. In co-dependency, relationship partners lose the ability to depend on and give each other support in a way that is mutually beneficial. Instead of forming a bond based on love, trust, and mutual respect, theirs is one based on neediness and unhealthy dependency.

Frequently this type of situation - one in which the codependent person is constantly self-sacrificing in increasingly desperate efforts to attain validation from a partner who may or may not be compliant - leads to a build-up of resentment and anger which serves only to compound the toxicity of the bond between the two and cause further self-loathing and loss of self esteem.

> "We rescue people from their responsibilities. We take care of people's responsibilities for them. Later, we get mad at them for what we've done. Then we feel used and sorry for ourselves. That is the pattern, the triangle."

— Melody Beattie, Author of 'Codependent No More: How to Stop Controlling Others and Start Caring for Yourself'

If left unaddressed, the symptoms of codependency tend to worsen over time and become ingrained habits which are more and more difficult to break. Although the narrative may play itself out differently in each relationship, these identifiable symptoms of codependent behavior are shared in common by most, if not all.

Characteristics of Codependency

Low self-esteem

Whether a person's lack of understanding of their self-worth precedes their involvement in a codependent relationship or not, that person will exhibit low self-esteem as part of and due to their involvement in the relationship's dysfunction. Loss of identity and the constant search for external validation keep codependents suspended in a perpetually hollow state where they can't value themselves because they are, to an extent, unaware that there is anything there to value.

Poor boundaries

A boundary is, by definition, a line that marks the limits of an area, or a dividing line between two areas. With regard to interpersonal relationships, a boundary has very much the same meaning: it refers to the implied division between two people defined as separate and distinct individuals. In codependent relationships where otherwise distinct individuals are intertwined or enmeshed with one another emotionally and psychologically, the boundaries which delineate between them become blurred and indistinct. It becomes difficult to distinguish which thoughts and feelings belong to which individual since codependents are so apt to assume responsibility for the feelings of others and conversely to inappropriately hold others accountable for their own emotions.

Dysfunctional ways of communicating

Codependents have great difficulty effectively and authentically communicating their thoughts, feelings, and needs. Due to habitually suppressing or ignoring those thoughts, feelings, and needs, they are frequently unable to identify what they even are. They can be very inaccurate in their perceptions of and reactions to thoughts expressed by other people, and sometimes, they're afraid to be truthful, because of the fear of upsetting someone else.

Difficulty saying "no"

Codependent individuals tend to have trouble saying "no" when asked to take on tasks or responsibilities, even when the assumption of those tasks is a significant inconvenience or hardship. Codependents will feel guilt at the thought of placing their own needs ahead of the wants of others. The compulsive need to help whenever possible, motivated by the 'need to be needed' and to garner approval can dispel all rational thought.

Dependency

One common thread amongst codependents is a fear of rejection or abandonment. They need constant reassurance that they are loved and accepted in order to feel good about themselves. Because of this, many feel that they need to always be in a relationship because they feel too unsettled and unsure of themselves being alone. This trait makes it very hard for them to end a relationship, even when the relationship is unhealthy, and they end up feeling they have no option but to stay and endure it.

Obsessiveness

The inherent fear and anxiety that underlie codependency can cause the people it affects to spend inordinate amounts of time and energy over-thinking. Other people or relationships are usually the focus. They can also become obsessed when they think they've made or might make a "mistake." Other times, they might become preoccupied with fantasies of how they'd like things to be or romanticize the past. Overall, the tendency to obsess is a form of avoidance and denial of what is really wrong in the present.

Fear of intimacy

Many people in codependent relationships are afraid to be too open and close with their partners. Emotional intimacy can be terrifying for someone who depends upon the approval of others to survive because the fear of being judged or rejected and then abandoned is just too great. They may also be afraid of being too close emotionally because they will be smothered by the relationship or the other partner. This leads some codependents to avoid intimacy by becoming "unavailable". This creates discord when, for example, one partner wants to spend more time together than the other partner does. In reality, one partner is denying a need for closeness while the other is denying a need for separateness.

Denial

One of the biggest problems for people living with codependency and the biggest reason they persist in their behavior even though they know something is not quite right is that they don't want to acknowledge that the label "codependent" could apply to them. They will either deny the very existence of any sort of problem or if they are able to admit that there is a problem, they believe that it is caused by someone else or by a particular situation. Codependents also deny their own feelings and needs. They either invalidate their emotions or simply can't identify what they are feeling and are more concerned anyway with what others are feeling. The same is true with regard to their needs. A codependent person will compulsively prioritize the needs of others while neglecting his or her own. Often, the person is unaware or in denial of what their needs even are.

Could you be codependent?

Ask yourself if you feel anxious when you deny someone - anyone you have a relationship with - something they have asked. Consider your reactions when someone disagrees with you or says something about you. Do you react to, or take personally, the thoughts and opinions of everyone regarding you? Think about the last time a friend of yours needed help. Did you feel guilty for not helping, even if they didn't ask? Or did you offer to help, then feel rejected when they said no?

Although you may acknowledge that you possess some of these traits to a degree, it does not necessarily mean that you are codependent. Codependency describes unhealthy **patterns** and extremes of thought and behavior with regard to interpersonal relationships. However, if you recognize that certain traits are leading you to engage in codependent behavior, making it difficult for you to relate to others, you might want to consider the possibility that you could be codependent and begin to take steps to address the issue.

Chapter 2: Types of Codependent Personalities and Behavior

Codependency can take many forms. There are a few different personality models that are indicative of codependency. There are also several types of codependent behavior, with each one highlighting different characteristics.

First, we'll look at four different personalities associated with codependency: the Martyr, the Savior, the Coach, and the Enabler.

The Martyr

A martyr, historically, is someone who is willing to sacrifice themselves for their beliefs. A martyr would be undesirable to government or religious leaders because the death of a martyr would bring attention to the message of the martyr - which was usually the corruption or immoral actions of the said government or religious leaders.

The modern meaning of a martyr is someone who unnecessarily sacrifices their own feelings or needs for someone else. This model personifies the codependent characteristic of extreme caretaking, the inability to say no, dependency, and obsessiveness. The Martyr also has a compulsive need to be "right" all the time and will often manipulate the situation they are in to meet that need. In exhibiting these traits, the martyr feeds the codependent relationship.

The Savior

The Savior codependent will often put themselves in a position where they are expected to (or claim that they "*have to*") fix a situation or person by taking on their problems as their own. They also tend to feel self-righteous because they "help" everyone and never ask for anything in return. The Savior might help the person that is in the adverse situation and take on the results as well-meaning. They take responsibility for what happens *after* they help, even though it is beyond their control.

The codependent savior needs the approval of the person they are helping, as well as anyone who may be affected by their help, and not getting it can generate feelings of inadequacy or depression. Additionally, if the Savior is unable to effectively help the person they are trying to, they may begin to feel unnecessary and either withdraw or act out irrationally.

The Savior personifies the dependency characteristic of co-dependency, along with extreme caretaking.

The Coach

The Coach codependent feels the need to insert themselves into others' lives to offer advice and talk them through the problems they are facing. The Coach will often exhibit controlling behavior, illustrate poor communication, or little regard for boundaries. They don't feel the need to hold back their advice and tend to push their views on others.

If the codependent Coach sees that their advice is not being utilized or listened to, they can easily become irritable and lash out, accusing the person they are trying to help of not being willing to better their situation by not listening or heeding advice born from their own experience. The codependent behavior feeds the Coach's need to feel important.

The Enabler

The Enabler is the codependent model that allows the other person in the relationship to have whatever and act however they like with no consequences. The Enabler will always be the one to "clean up" behind the other person, but not hold them responsible or encourage them to change their behavior, regardless of how unhealthy the behavior may be. They might give money to someone with a drug addiction, make excuses for poor behavior, or simply tolerates the actions of another person.

When an Enabler is engaging in their codependent behavior, they often feel as though they are helpless to change the situation or the person causing the situation. They assume the role of victim, claiming they can't do anything to stop the problem, only negate the effects caused. They either don't understand or deny that their actions are encouraging the unhealthy behavior in the other person, so they don't see how they can change anything.

The Enabler will exhibit low self-esteem, extreme caretaking, the inability to say no, and denial regarding their part in the others' behavior.

Behaviors

The following is an overview of five common types of codependent behavior but is by no means a comprehensive survey of all behaviors associated with codependency. All relationships, like all individuals, are unique and not everyone follows the same pattern. However, in most relationships where codependency is present, all of these behaviors are evident to some degree.

Controlling

"A codependent person is one who has let another person's behavior affect him or her and who is obsessed with controlling that person's behavior."

— *Melody Beattie, Author of 'Codependent No More: How to Stop Controlling Others and Start Caring for Yourself'*

Control – whether over oneself or others, whether taken or given away – is one of the most significant hallmarks of codependency. Having a sense of control can make codependents feel both safe and empowered but it can limit their ability to live an authentic life when they try to maintain that sense of control by shutting themselves off from their true feelings. It also makes it difficult for them to refrain from violating the boundaries of other people, and next to impossible to successfully navigate interpersonal conflict. Still, people who are codependent don't know how else to operate.

Codependents exhibit a controlling mindset with regard to their consistent prioritization of the needs of other people over their own. They perpetually deny themselves the things they want, and forcibly suppress any unpleasant feelings that arise as a result. In many cases, codependents will develop coping mechanisms involving self-medication (such as alcoholism or drug addiction) or compulsive behaviors (such as workaholism) to avoid or dull the pain that stems from their self-punishment and so they don't have to really feel any frustration, anger, or resentment at their self-neglect. By remaining in control of themselves and their emotions, they are equipped to then exert control over other people and situations.

In the mind of someone who is codependent, it becomes necessary to dictate almost every aspect of every facet of every action or interaction with everybody close to them. They need others to behave the way they want them to behave in order to feel as though everything is literally under control. This means that they have little to no respect for boundaries – either their own or those of others - and can alternate between being overbearing or bossy and inappropriately self-effacing, sometimes, within the same conversation. Both approaches are blatantly manipulative.

Codependent people often struggle to effectively resolve problems between themselves and others due to an inherent lack of assertiveness fostered by their low self-esteem. This, coupled with their inability to constructively express their personal needs and wants, can cause them to choose to either defer and relinquish control when disagreeing with others, thus passively ensuring their needs will be denied, or seize full control of the situation by manipulating others into fulfilling their roles as assigned in the codependent's agenda. It's always a win or lose scenario and never an equitable compromise, meaning that one party or the other is always left feeling resentful, which is not a positive outcome.

Enabling

Enabling is another type of behavior which typically manifests in codependency. It refers specifically to the way in which one person in a relationship will justify or excuse the bad behavior or bad choices of the other person. The classic example of this is when the spouse of an alcoholic overlooks the other partner's alcoholism and actively tries to shield him or her from the consequences of his or her actions. The codependent spouse allows or 'enables' the alcoholic to continue being addicted without having to face any potential repercussions. In codependent relationships, this behavior extends beyond just situations involving addiction or alcoholism to include any situation in which the enabled person is not being held responsible for their weakness, inadequacy, or irresponsibility.

The codependent enabler may believe he or she is helping by sheltering the enabled person from painful reality, but the truth is that by absolving the enabled of accountability for his or her actions, the enabler is sentencing him or her to remain trapped within the dysfunctional behavior pattern with no way out. There can be no change and no growth until the enabled person is forced (or allowed) to confront the truth.

The codependent is acting out of a sincere desire to protect their wayward spouse, friend, parent, or child from harm but does not understand that instead of helping, their actions serve to exacerbate and compound the existing problem. Codependents have a combination of poor boundaries, low self-esteem, and an overwhelming 'need to be needed,' all of which fuel their tendency to want to solve problems for other people regardless of whether or not it is appropriate for them to do so. In addition, they show a seeming inability to disengage from someone they feel compelled to help, regardless of the circumstances. Even when the other person is specifically refusing the help offered, the codependent will persist, reluctant to acknowledge that their help is unwanted because, in their mind, that would constitute rejection. It is for this reason that the codependent cannot see how their enabling behavior does not help the enabled person overcome problems and may, in fact, contribute to making things worse.

People-pleasing

People-pleasing behavior directly relates to the codependent's constant yearning for external validation. Approval and acceptance from others are necessary in order for them to feel secure. They can't easily tolerate anyone being upset or critical of them and to avoid this, they will be willing to do whatever is asked of them in order to win approval and avert judgment.

Codependent people-pleasers feel distressed at the thought of saying "no" to anyone out of fear that they will be perceived negatively. Even if what they are being asked to do will put an undue strain on them, or are objectively unreasonable or impossible, they will feel guilt at even the idea of placing their own needs ahead of those of others. Often, people who fall into this pattern of behavior will overload themselves with activities and overcommit their time. This can lead to resentment which the codependent will not be able to dismiss. Since they cannot reconcile with their guilt over saying "no," they will become trapped into painful compliance. If not, they will worry that they will be regarded as selfish, lazy, uncaring, and a generally undesirable person. The anxiety about receiving this sort of "bad review" and the rejection it implies compels them to go to great lengths to never have to disappoint others by opting not to agree to their requests.

Though on the surface people-pleasing behavior may seem selfless, it really isn't. Like much of typical codependent behavior, it is a means to the desired end – namely, asserting control over people and situations. If the desired outcome is to gain favor and invite praise from other people, what better way to obtain it than to willingly devote all your time and energy to helping advance their personal goals, even at the expense of your own?

Codependent people can be passive people-pleasers too, by refusing to state a preference when asked, reflexively deferring to someone else's opinions even if they oppose your own or settling for less so that others can have more. As with refusing to say "no," the refusal to say "yes" is motivated by the same need for approval and both are employed as tools of emotional manipulation

When this type of behavior enters into interactions between two people in a close relationship, it can lead to misunderstanding, the breakdown of communication, and harboring of resentment. Over time, this will compromise the health of the relationship and of the individual partners themselves.

Self-denigrating

To denigrate is to belittle, dismiss, or devalue. To self-denigrate is then to perpetrate a harshly critical attitude toward oneself. In codependency, self- denigrating can start when the codependent offers help to the other person in the relationship, and the other person rejects their help. The codependent would feel inadept, inadequate, or possibly in the way of the other person. The codependent would repress those feelings around the other person in hopes that their feelings wouldn't be found out and validated. Eventually, the codependent will feel useless in the relationship. This can either lead the codependent to fall into depression or cause them to become even more enmeshed in the relationship to find their approval.

Self-denigration in codependency should not be confused with not being able to accept a compliment or other praise. Most people are modest and find it difficult to acknowledge their successes due to the ingrained habit, but self-denigration is much harsher than simple modesty. Self-denigration is also different from self-deprecation in that denigration doesn't have that humor element, and depreciation is expressing disapproval as opposed to denigration's purpose of criticism and defamation. When a codependent uses self-denigration, they are feeding into their compulsive need for approval and further damaging their already low self- worth.

Overreacting

Codependents tend to overreact to any opinion given about them, regardless of the source or truth behind it. They take everything personally, without consideration of context. Overreaction to stimulus feeds into the obsessive part of the codependent's personality and, in most cases, the low self- esteem as well. A codependent that is overreacting doesn't recognize the boundaries of another person's thoughts or feelings. They just automatically assume that any vague comment is a response to them as a person, making the commenter's problems theirs instead of seeing the commenter as having an issue that is totally unrelated to the codependent.

As is the case in codependent behavior in general, overreacting to a situation or person is a learned behavior. The codependent has seen others in conditions that they believe to be associated with what they are facing and replicate the reactions they've seen or experienced before. The codependent has unconsciously decided that what they are experiencing in the present moment is the same as the last experience, though they may not be related, or the memory is flawed in some way or incomplete (such as in the case of seeing their mother reacting to something regarding their father, when they don't truly know what's happening.) Overreacting is the only way the codependent knows how to respond.

These personality models and behaviors are not exclusive to codependency, nor is this an exhaustive list of what to expect with a codependent individual. There is any number of combinations of behaviors and personalities that a codependent may exhibit. These personalities are built on previous experience and family life. A codependent person can often cover up and make excuses for their behavior and has learned over the course of their lives to pretend and repress their emotions in favor of focusing on others, making it difficult to accurately diagnose codependency from the outside looking in.

Chapter 3: Trauma, Healing, and Forgiveness

Like all behaviors, codependency has a beginning point. The codependent has learned (usually from the adults in the caretaking position) how to act and has modeled their behavior after what they have seen. Distressing events contribute to codependent behaviors, be they from abuse or death or any number of events in a person's life. It is possible to move out of the codependent cycle, and this chapter will examine the purpose of self-awareness and self-acceptance as beginning steps to doing just that as well as identify how co-dependency is initiated in individuals.

What causes codependency to develop in the first place?

As stated earlier, codependency was first recognized as a behavior associated with families of addicts- probably because addiction is a dependence on something extrinsic, so it makes sense that *codependent* behavior would be most apparent there. When codependency became widely recognized, families of addicts generally were used to keeping secrets and repressing their needs in order to appear "perfect" to the outsider and from there, developed as a lifetime habit. Codependency began in dysfunctional families by the families not being open about their feelings and needs or allowing their emotional identities to develop. Families of addicts or mentally incapacitated individuals would feel ashamed of their families and welcomed the encouragement to keep their problems hidden away from public scrutiny.

In recent history, codependency has been studied more in-depth. Now, we have a better idea of how it develops, manifests, and heal. It can still begin in dysfunctional families, but now, it is known that codependency can also begin in friendships and romantic relationships as well. Codependency is half of a codependent relationship, and the behaviors have to be learned somehow in order for them to be put into action. A person may be predisposed to codependent behavior or have been through trauma that creates the behaviors. A codependent person may be codependent in one particular relationship, or they can display their behaviors throughout all relationships in their lives.

In general, codependency begins during childhood. It usually occurs when a child has to attend to the household in ways that are beyond their years and capabilities, such as cooking dinner or ensuring that their siblings are ready for school on time, or as a result of some sort of trauma, such as a drug-addicted or mentally ill parent or death of an important family member. Sometimes, a child is looked upon by the adults in their lives as confidantes or is made to fill the narcissistic void in one or both parents. Filling in where the guardians are failing usurps their energy and emotional wellbeing. Thus, their needs begin to fall to the wayside in place of taking care of everyone else. While codependent behaviors may be essential in childhood, carrying the behaviors to adulthood can mean difficult or failing relationships.

Codependency may also have roots in abusive relationships, either child or adult, which is quite traumatic to either age group. If a codependent is in an emotionally abusive relationship, they may force themselves to change who they are in order to keep the peace or live up to the abuser's expectations. The codependent may not protect children in the home from the abuse, believing that they can't do anything to stop it or lessen it, and thereby, becoming complicit without meaning to.

In cases where a codependent is the primary caregiver, codependent behavior can be caused by the forming habit of control, especially if the caregiver role is presented suddenly and without warning. The caregiver is the one to dress, bathe, feed, encourage, transport, and make decisions for their charge. Over time, this control can be hard to let go of since the caregiver no longer sees the boundary lines between where their assistance is needed and the ways that their charge is able to care for themselves. Before the caregiver role is needed, the codependent may not ever exhibit signs of codependent behaviors or personality but may evolve through their new role.

Self-awareness and self-acceptance

The codependent individual may not be aware of their behaviors and tendencies. In order to change the behavior, the codependent must first recognize the signs and symptoms in themselves and then accept that they engage in these behaviors for whatever reasons they see.

Once the codependent begins to recognize their behaviors, they will need to analyze themselves and see which behaviors are to the extreme, and which ones are purely caring behaviors with no undertones of codependency. They have to become self-aware of what they are saying and doing that encourages the unhealthy behavior of their partner, family member, or friend. Self-awareness may not happen all at once. It may happen in stages depending on how close the codependent person pays attention to themselves and their actions. If a codependent person only recognizes one behavior at a time, it could take a while to seek treatment for their tendencies. Adding on to the process of becoming self-aware, some codependents may be in denial of their behavior. They feel that they are not addicted to drugs, or they are responsible (*too* responsible, even) for their loved one's behavior of immaturity or chronic underachievement. These codependents still have not fully achieved self-awareness. A requirement for self-awareness is to listen for negative self-talk and discover how to turn that negative voice off. When you can recognize the negativity your subconscious is creating in your mind, you can then begin to break it down and raise your self-esteem.

After the initial awareness happens, the codependent will then have to work on accepting themselves and their flaws. This may be especially difficult for the Coach or the Savior because these two personality models inherently believe they are only "helping" their loved one and not being codependent. They may not be able to recognize when they are participating in the codependent behavior or could be in denial since the addictive behavior is not their own. However, when a codependent person is ready to break the cycle and stop enabling their partner, recognizing the signs of codependency will become easier. A codependent person may very well need the assistance of a therapist or counselor to help them identify the unhealthy behavior and accept that they have faults to be corrected. For many, accepting personal fault is difficult merely because they don't want to face the fact that they may not have all the answers. Self-acceptance is not easy for anyone facing adverse feelings about their actions. Acceptance isn't about changing the behavior; it is only meant for a codependent to understand their flaws. When a codependent accepts themselves, a path is opened up that was previously closed due to fighting the situation and new feelings begin to emerge- feelings of compassion toward oneself and the ability to soothe the negative feelings that accompany the denial. Often, once a codependent accepts their personalities, they begin to put less weight on others' opinions on them and their obsessive need to please in order to turn the opinions positive.

Both of these are emotionally difficult and draining processes to go through. If not because of the recognition that a codependent is not perfect, then possibly because of the realization that they have to change what are essentially ingrained habits and behaviors. They will face analyzing all of their mannerisms that could be enabling the other person in their relationship and be forced to stay aware of the ways they are contributing to the unhealthy actions of others; acknowledging and accepting one's part in permitting detrimental activities of an addict or other misbehavior is sometimes heartrending. However, accepting the faults and getting past the denial is the first step on the road to recovery.

Paths to Recovery

After the critical steps of self-awareness and self-acceptance, the path to recovering from codependent behaviors and personality opens up and becomes more accessible. A codependent person can begin to see ways to not only break the cycles but begin to heal so they can avoid co-dependency in the future.

The codependent must learn to detach themselves from their loved one in order to be able to begin to heal. They have to learn how to separate the person from the addictive or unhealthy behavior. The codependent also has to learn to let go of the feeling of responsibility for the unhealthy behavior; they can't control their loved one (despite their obsessive desire to do so), and they can't control the outcome of their loved one's decisions. Detachment does not mean abandonment - it is important to remember that, both for the codependent and the addict. Detachment is meant to allow for boundaries to be set and to be able to see the big picture situation instead of taking care to get rid of little mistakes. Detachment offers the codependent the opportunity to step back and view the situation a bit more objectively than they could before. The detachment also means that the partner in the relationship can begin to understand how to make their own decisions and see how those decisions affect their lives from that point on. This way, the partner can gain confidence in themselves and have that knowledge that they are strong enough to overcome their unhealthy behaviors.

The key in any addictive and recovery situation is forgiveness. The codependent has to recognize in themselves their flaws and their function in the continuation of damaging actions in the other person in their relationship. Along with this recognition, the codependent needs to understand how forgiveness works and what it means for themselves and the other person in their relationship. Forgiveness of oneself is most important - the codependent should forgive themselves in order to move forward in overcoming the behavior associated with their codependency to ensure that they can no longer facilitate their loved one's acts in addiction. A codependent also must forgive the addict for taking advantage of them in order to let go of any resentment which will hold them back from being able to move on from their previous behaviors and focus on their futures.

It is important to note here that simply saying that a codependent forgives is not the same as *actually* forgiving the wrongs that have been committed, either from the codependent toward themselves or from the addict. Forgiveness is a process, a series of actions that have to be worked through. Similarly, forgiveness is a difficult process and one that may not happen right away. It's ok for a codependent to acknowledge hurt and anger and take the time they need to process it in order to feel ready to forgive. A codependent should try to understand that the behavior and actions had a purpose and try to find and understand that purpose. With that understanding comes the acknowledgment of the feelings and letting them go with the new determination of setting limits and being kind to oneself.

When a codependent is learning self-awareness, self-acceptance, and forgiveness, they may feel as though the emotions and feelings are insurmountable and that they will be feeling hurt and/or angry for a long time. However, emotions come in waves (scientifically studied, emotions last around 60 seconds) and once the wave has passed, the codependent should be able to decide to let go of the pain. This is not to say that they once again allow the other person in their relationship to continue to behave as they have been, it simply means that the codependent is willing to move forward in a healthier way than they have previously been doing. Instead of continuing to allow the behavior, the codependent can now learn to build and maintain boundaries to encourage self-respect and self-worth. Now, in place of forcing the emotional energy to manage and control or clean up the other person's behavior, the codependent can feel the less draining emotions of peace and serenity, which are needed in order to foster self-respect. Forgiveness will allow the codependent to feel powerful and grow stronger in recovery.

Forgiveness is the trailhead on the path to recovery from co-dependency. Between these three steps, a codependent can begin to heal their past hurts and truly keep their help to actual *help* as opposed to dependency.

Chapter 4: Beginning to Heal

Healing requires awareness, acceptance, and forgiveness as discussed in the previous chapter. For some codependents, they may be able to begin the healing process on their own, but for most, they need guidance from a trained outside source such as a therapist. A therapist can walk the codependent through the work needed to recover and heal.

Once the awareness of the behavior becomes apparent, and the codependent finds their path to healing, their road is just beginning. A commitment to recovery takes work. As is true of any behavior changes, a conscious effort is required and must be consistent in order to stay on track. However, the codependent shouldn't be too hard on themselves if they stumble or have setbacks. The codependent didn't learn the behavior overnight, so unlearning it won't happen overnight, either.

Recognizing Unhealthy Behavior Patterns

Since codependent behaviors first begin in childhood, most therapies involve exploring the relationships from the codependent's childhood and their experiences. Psychoanalysis is often used to examine the behaviors and psychotherapy is the norm for treatment due to the difficult nature in changing ingrained habits and behaviors.

Treatment begins with awareness, as earlier stated. Recognizing the unhealthy behaviors individually is the first step but recognizing the behavior *patterns* may come a bit later, once awareness has been established and practiced. It is crucial to differentiate between codependent behaviors and codependent behavior patterns. Codependent behaviors exist in a wider range than most realize but displaying some codependent behaviors is not always indicative of codependency. Codependent patterns are more suggestive of a codependent personality.

Therapy can help the codependent figure out their patterns, but the codependent has to be the one to stay aware of when they happen and which situations most trigger the behavior patterns. The codependent needs to be willing to go from simply being aware of the behavior patterns to doing something to alter them.

Acknowledging that a codependent has adverse behaviors is where the healing begins. Next, identifying the pattern of behavior lights the pathway. Some people can stay aware of their patterns, but others need some visualization. A therapist may suggest writing or journaling about the patterns and behavior, and there are worksheets available to help keep track of the patterns and keep them in the forefront of one's mind. Writing or using worksheets can help with the next part of healing, which is developing mindfulness.

Developing Mindfulness

Mindfulness goes beyond being aware of your thoughts, actions, and responses. Being mindful includes paying attention to our mannerisms and responses when we interact with the outside stimuli we encounter. This is done without being judgmental of ourselves, just purely noticing in an objective way. Most of the thoughts and self-talk we experience comes from a negative place in the mind. Becoming mindful means that you are able to look at those thoughts without putting yourself down or criticizing yourself. It means that you can see where your negativity comes from. Being mindful isn't focused on "fixing" yourself, only observing yourself.

When a person is learning mindfulness, they will also be learning how to let go of control. A codependent person has an extremely difficult time deferring control to someone else. This is why it is so critical for a codependent to learn mindfulness - it teaches a codependent how to look, observe, and notice what is happening while not forcing their own opinions or actions on the situation. A mindful person can look and see what their good aspects are; a codependent person will have a hard time with this because they don't want to look inside themselves and see what is making them tick. A codependent may see self-reflection as useless or "stupid" because they are afraid of what they may find.

With this in mind, being mindful is achievable in small ways. Think of yourself using compassionate thoughts - *"My obsessive thinking about an incident two days ago is only a habit."; "I stop the thoughts and bring myself back into the present."; "I will eventually have reshaped how I think and feel about situations."* You will see over time that the last statement has come true. It takes patience and practice to reach this new thought pattern, but mindfulness will help attain it. Although you may not believe it in the beginning, these little thoughts will become reflexive instead of the negative thoughts that you are experiencing now. Each new instance of awareness helps feed into the automaticity of the new thoughts. Be mindful of how you are responding to the world and the things that you come across.

Much of the difficulty of seeking treatment for codependency is that the things that form the personality of a codependent are the things that have to be changed about them. They are taking what they are, what they know, and having to reshape it into a healthier version. Not only is behavior modification difficult, but it is also hurtful to learn that everything about you is in some way damaged or damaging to others. When considering codependency treatment from this perspective, it's easy to see why recovery is a difficult process.

Even if you are just starting out on your recovery, you are able to change your thought patterns and your personality. Remember that your behavior didn't develop overnight, so it won't be changed overnight either. A codependent is only now learning how to use the compassion muscle, and until the muscle is strengthened, it can't become reflexive. Mindfulness is not about being critical of yourself or trying to change the behavior - this is important to remember! - but only for observation.

Inevitably, there will be tests to the codependent's recovery. In that situation, the codependent should take a step back, take a deep breath, and allow the reflex emotions to cool so that awareness can take its place. This gives the codependent the opportunity to practice their mindfulness. Taking this one second to breathe stops the unconscious reactions and engages mindfulness and giving yourself the choice on how you react or respond.

Thich Nhat Hanh suggests that conscious breathing helps with staying in the moment when feelings and emotions become overwhelming. Taking conscious breaths makes the codependent pause and think before giving in to their instinctual behavior. It also has the added benefit of putting your body into a peaceful state as opposed to the panic state that the body feels naturally when you're breathing shallow and quick.

Using conscious breathing techniques also take practice, but employing the techniques is beneficial in achieving mindfulness. People generally breathe in from their chests, not their abdomens. Begin your breathing practice by placing your hand around your belly button and inhale through your nose, feeling your abdomen expand. Then, once the belly and torso are expanded, exhale and contract all the muscles until there is little or no breath left. This will help calm panic, gain perspective, pause the instinctual behaviors, and provide grounding if you're feeling over anxious.

The codependent person tries to control everything around them in the hopes of gaining approval from the people who matter to them. However, in becoming mindful, the codependent is making it possible to practice letting go; using phrases like "That's not my job to fix," or "I'm sure your decision will be a good one," encourages them to give control of the situation to the person who *should* be in charge - the person who is creating the problem with their behavior. The codependent cannot take responsibility for the actions of others, as has been stated earlier.

The codependent may find themselves angry with the other person in the relationship due to repeated, intentional adverse behavior. In this case, mindfulness can be helpful in catching the reflexive reaction of yelling or crying. Using mindfulness here may be as simple as a physical release such as exercise or breathing techniques to overcome the wave of anger.

A symptom of codependency is depression, which is another form of anger. Except, depression is anger turned on oneself. Mindfulness in dealing with depression can help keep the codependent out of the downward spiral of depression. Writing and reading about depression encourages mindfulness with regard to the signs of depression. The codependent can use mindfulness to keep from falling into the trap of obsessive thinking and denial in the form of substance abuse or working non-stop.

A codependent person also suffers considerable guilt for reasons that are sometimes either unknown or unfounded. Being mindful of when that guilt begins and the trigger for it can help assuage the guilt or point out the irrationality of it. The codependent can ask if they would want anyone of their friends or family to feel as guilty as they do all the time, or think about the cause of the guilt - is it legitimately something that is a result of the codependent's actions, or is the codependent taking on the guilt from someone else? The codependent will also need to practice saying "no" when the other person in the relationship makes demands on them, and not feel guilty about it. One key lesson to learn in a codependent's recover is that they are not responsible for the happiness or productivity of anyone besides themselves - not to mention, the codependent needs to draw boundaries for the other person in the relationship to begin to take care of themselves. Mindfulness is not just for the codependent, but also for the other person to learn as well.

Mindfulness is another step on the path of recovery. Mindfulness opens the heart and mind to accept oneself as they are and leads them to learn to love themselves.

Learning to Love Yourself

Codependency often results from the codependent not receiving the love and attention needed for proper emotional growth. Along with not receiving the love they need, the codependent has no reference for what it looks like when someone loves themselves. Thus, they can't love themselves in the way they need in order to avoid the codependent behaviors that seek out approval.

When a codependent seeks treatment, the therapist works to try and get the codependent to learn what healthy love looks like and how to turn it inward. This, like mindfulness, takes practice to gain automaticity of positive feelings over the negative feelings that are inherently associated with codependency.

Loving oneself starts with being able to appreciate silence and alone time. So often, the codependent avoids being alone with themselves for fear of negative thoughts creeping up. Once the codependent doesn't have to spend energy on filling silence or learns to say no, they can begin to appreciate themselves because they are no longer focused on everything around them. They are now focused on their own thoughts and feelings. Alone time coupled with mindfulness tends to lead to a stronger sense of self and a stronger ability to alter codependent behaviors.

Additionally, learning to love oneself and be okay alone makes way for the codependent learning to ask for help when needed, and do so without lingering feelings of guilt or distress over not being able to control their environment. Many codependents don't feel as though they deserve help or don't want to be a burden. Unfortunately, many codependents don't consider that their friends being able to help them may allow friends to feel valued and closer to the codependent. Moreover, asking for help meeting the things that a codependent can't do on their own, for example, intimacy can circumvent feelings of resentment in the future when another person doesn't meet the needs of the codependent; the codependent expects the other person in the relationship to just *know* what they need without voicing it.

Loving oneself means taking care of oneself. Many times, codependents are so focused on the other person in the relationship or the other people around them in general that they don't realize that they need something themselves. Physical needs and emotional needs are just as important to meet for the codependent as it is for the people they usually take care of.

Needs manifest in different ways. Relaxation is necessary, and having fun pursuing hobbies or pleasurable activities fulfills a need beyond the basic survival needs. Laughter eases stress and creates endorphins which foster positive feelings and self-love. Pleasure also helps to boost energy.

Loving yourself also means protecting yourself from abuse - both physical and emotional. You wouldn't want another loved one being on the receiving end of abuse, so allowing yourself to be in that position is just as bad. You can't love yourself if you're not standing up for yourself or letting someone you care about tear down your soul.

Another part of being mindful and learning to love yourself is being kind to yourself. Change the tone of your inner voice to be gentler with yourself. Teach your inner voice to be encouraging and praising.

The path to healing from codependency is just that - a path. It is full of twists and turns, beginning with self-awareness and recognizing unhealthy behavior patterns. In order to stay on that path, a codependent should be mindful of their reactions and responses to outside stimuli and learn to love themselves. These things at the beginning of the path will lay the foundation to true healing.

Accepting Your Partner

In a codependent relationship, the codependent was attracted to their partner because there was something about them that they could "fix." The codependent is attracted to people who are emotionally unstable or are not fully in control of their lives. The codependent looks for those relationships so they can fulfill the need from their childhood for feeling needed and having someone to center their life around. A codependent in a healthy relationship will not have their needs met and the relationship will not last.

The codependent will try to take control of the dependent person in the relationship in order to fix what's wrong with them. Unfortunately, the codependent in the relationship will be taking on all the responsibility of the dependent's actions and will quickly become stressed and burned out with the dependent. Even though the codependent may realistically understand that they cannot fix the dependent, they nevertheless try and force the dependent to change. Despite technically knowing that the dependent will not change until they are ready, the codependent still believes and pushes that the dependent will change if they love the codependent enough and recognize how their behavior is affecting the codependent.

The dependent may go along with the codependent's rules for a while, but ultimately, will fall back into their old patterns. The codependent will continue the pattern of control and responsibility while continuing to wish the dependent would change.

Once the codependent decides to change their behavior for a healthy pattern, they will have to learn to accept the dependent as they are until the dependent decides they are ready for change - *if* it ever happens. Learning mindfulness is a good start on this path, along with setting boundaries and learning to let go of the control the codependent so seeks in relationships. The codependent has a long road ahead of them for accepting themselves and changing their behavior; learning to accept their partner will be no less daunting. However, there is a method suggested by Joshua Millburn and Ryan Nicodemus called the TARA method - a four-step process of accepting others as they are without judgment. The TARA method states that acceptance of others is made easier when the codependent follows these four principles:

<u>Tolerate</u> the other's quirks. The codependent might find the behaviors that are characteristic of the dependent somewhat annoying or off-putting, but they are part of what makes up the dependent. However, the codependent entered the relationship knowing that there are some things about the other person that make them unique. They need to learn to tolerate these things in order to move forward with acceptance.

<u>Accept</u> that these things will always exist. If the codependent is choosing to accept the dependent, they choose to accept the whole person, not only some parts. After all, the codependent is learning that they can't change the dependent, so they will simply have to learn to accept the behaviors.

<u>Respect</u> the dependent's need for these quirks. For example, if the dependent needs to alphabetize their DVD collection, the codependent will have to respect that need and allow them to do it.

Note: this principle does not apply if the dependent is a drug abuser. In these cases, the codependent should seek professional help in managing the codependent's feelings about the dependent's need for the dependent's drug use so as not to encourage drug use.

Appreciate that the dependent is unique, with unique needs and characteristics. Turn the negative annoyance about the dependent's quirk into a positive thought. This requires conscious effort at first but retraining the brain to appreciate the things that make the dependent different will allow the codependent to move past the annoying behavior instead of focusing on it. As long as the dependent is in the codependent's life, the dependent's quirks will be, too.

Accepting the dependent as they are will go a long way in healing the relationship. It makes way for establishing trust and a non-judgmental relationship, which is needed for both partners to feel emotionally healthy. It is another way to encourage the codependent to let go of some of the control they thrive on and find other ways to have their needs met or get practice refocusing that energy toward something else in the codependent's life.

If you're enjoying this book, I would appreciate it if you went to the place of purchase and left a short positive review. Thank you

Chapter 5: Changing Codependent Relationships

Chapter 4 looked at changing the pattern of codependent behavior. When change happens, it has to start with one person, the person who wants the change. Trying to change someone without changing oneself is ineffective and unlikely.

The codependent has begun to change themselves. Normally, this results from the codependent having hit rock bottom, the point in their lives or relationships which they feel they can no longer function the way they have been up to that point. Now that the codependent has started working on themselves, they must start working on the relationships that have them feeling as though they are at rock bottom.

Changing the codependent relationship requires patience and time, just as changing the codependent behavior patterns. Changing the relationship takes both people in the relationship in making a commitment to healing in order to keep the other person in their lives.

Relationship changes first begin with communication. The people in the relationship must learn to talk to one another and respond in healthy and sympathetic ways. But communication isn't just talking to one another; it requires listening and reading body language as well.

Developing Empathic Communication

When the term "empathic" is used, one thinks of feeling what others are feeling. This is also the case with codependent relationships. In healing a codependent relationship, both partners have to be willing to step into the shoes of the other person, to feel what they are feeling. Empathic communication means that the codependent is not only actively listening to the other person, but also is to understand how they feel and responding in a way they would want someone to respond to them if they were feeling the same.

Developing empathic communication involves three stages: sensing, processing, and responding. Each stage is the building block for the next, so you can't respond empathically without having first sensed what the other is feeling.

The first stage is sensing what the other person is feeling. This is not only listening to what they are saying, but also listening to what they are *not* saying, both with words and body language. *Sensing* implies that the listener is using cues like body language, the tone of voice, and facial expression to read the speaker's intent. The first step in empathic listening, this is the part of the process which allows the listener to interpret what the speaker is saying and is the beginning point in building the necessary skills to make empathic listening a frequently used skill. The listener has to be sensitive to what the other person is saying, understand how they feel, and pay attention to what the other person is implying as well as what they are saying.

The second stage of empathic listening is processing. In this stage, the listener is processing what the speaker is saying along with their other nonverbal cues to create the whole picture of the speaker's message. The listener demonstrates that the speaker's message is sticking with them by repeating the main points and confirming that they will remember what the speaker is saying.

The third and final stage of empathic listening is responding to the speaker. The listener has to prove to the speaker that they were listening and that they understood what the speaker was trying to impart. In this stage, if the listener doesn't understand nor needs clarification, they ask questions and summarize what the speaker said to ensure they completely comprehend the speaker's message. The responding stage includes using body language and eye contact to show the speaker that you are absorbing their message.

Empathic listening in a codependent relationship is essential to healing the relationship and making it a healthy one. The codependent person needs to feel heard in their needs and the dependent person needs to be able to express their needs, so they don't feel that they have to turn to the unhealthy behaviors in order to avoid feeling whatever is fueling their need for the behavior in the first place.

When a codependent relationship is in recovery, empathic listening assures both partners that they are heard and understood. Healing one's feelings helps to prevent future behavior patterns that are unhealthy and codependent in nature. Empathic listening is not always meant to "fix" the problems that the speaker is voicing; sometimes, simply listening and understanding is healing in itself. Empathic listening listens with the full body - body, mind, and spirit. Think of how it feels to really know you're being heard. The listener is open and engaged, and the speaker is gaining confidence in their message. Now, imagine how the other partner would feel when they truly know they are being heard. This is healing.

The codependent relationship often is not focused on what the partner truly needs, but instead on what the dependent partner needs and what the codependent partner projects onto the dependent partner. Neither of these situations meets the needs of the relationship. However, when empathic listening is employed, the partners learn to read one another in deeper, more meaningful ways. They can learn just the tiniest nuances of a facial expression to see through the façade of strength the other partner is trying to illustrate, and help their partner reach the point where they are no longer pretending strength but actually *being* strong.

When the partners in a codependent relationship feel that they are not being heard, it adds to the stress of the relationship, straining it further.

Conversely, when empathetic listening becomes more apparent, both partners feel more satisfaction in the relationship, and individuals with empathy are better able to manage conflict (mostly because they can put themselves in the shoes of the other person.)

Listening empathically doesn't apply only to listening to both partners in a relationship, but also listening to oneself. If a codependent listens empathically to themselves, they are better able to be mindful of themselves and their feelings. When one is empathic with their own thoughts, they are also more capable of listening empathically to others.

Empathic listening and communication are a solid foundation for a healthy relationship. It promotes healing and respect and builds trust between the people in the relationship.

Nurturing Mutual Respect

It should go without saying that a healthy relationship involves mutual respect between the partners. Unfortunately, mutual respect is frequently discarded in codependent relationships. In order to heal and recover from codependency and a codependent relationship, respect must be reestablished and nurtured. Many in a codependent relationship may not understand how to do this - either the codependent or the dependent. For both, the relationship is built on neediness and seeking the other person out for unhealthy intentions instead of being with a person for their personality.

For the codependent in the relationship, their desire is to control the other person and get them to do as they want them to do - this is not respect. This is manipulation. For the dependent in the relationship, they want the codependent to do something for them but often go about demanding it in a way that is disrespectful and manipulative. Moving past this detrimental element of the relationship requires both partners to learn respect. The interactions between the two people in the relationship generally are not done out of respect but some ulterior motive. Codependent relationships habitually put respect on the backburner as opposed to making respect a priority.

When the people in a codependent relationship begin turning their relationship around, they must understand that respect is mutual and not argue that they will give respect when they get it. This is not the way to a healthy relationship. Even if the codependent partner is the one to initiate the changes, the dependent partner must also be willing to change and offer respect. *Mutual* respect is both given and received between the partners.

Part of giving and receiving respect is setting and sticking to boundaries. Of course, the dependent and the codependent must respect themselves as well as one another, so they are obligated to pay attention to and obey the boundaries set by the other in the relationship as well as the ones set by themselves. After all, if you don't respect your own boundaries, how can you expect anyone else to? If the codependent isn't valuing themselves enough to recognize their own needs, they cannot fully heal and change their behavior patterns. They have to nurture their own self-respect without guilt.

On the same token, a codependent must also treat their partner's boundaries as important as well. Respect is fostered through listening and agreeing to value one another's needs and meet them as best they can.

Establishing Trust

A regular aspect of a codependent relationship is that trust between the partners in a codependent relationship is either non-existent or conditional (i.e., I only trust you if you come straight home from work and don't talk to any female friends.) Codependents and dependents use manipulation in place of trust. They believe that by making the other person do what they want, they won't have to think about how much they doubt the other person's intentions or behaviors. Codependents rarely trust anyone - whether it is trusting them to take care of themselves and make good decisions, or trusting someone not to abandon them. Their personalities simply do not have a place for trust. The dependent in the relationship regularly acts or says things that inspire distrust instead of belief in their abilities. Therefore, the codependent is validated in their belief in the need to take control over the relationship and continue their codependent behavior.

Part of being on the path to recovery from codependency is learning to let go of the obsessive need to control others and establish trust in them. While some people (dependents) need help along the way of becoming a healthier individual, most people are capable of taking care of themselves and handling their consequences. For the codependent, allowing the dependent to take on own responsibilities is extremely difficult. They often tell themselves, "Well, they haven't been able to _____ before, so they won't be able to now," or "They don't know how to ____ the right way." The codependent doesn't trust the dependent to learn from their mistakes or be able to figure out how to properly handle adult situations.

In order for the dependent to heal, they should learn how to take responsibilities for their own actions and behaviors. Otherwise, they will never understand how their behavior affects others and impacts their own lives. The codependent frequently doesn't understand this. They feel that the dependent won't be responsible, so they assume the consequences.

Codependents can hold the dependent back from healing, just as the dependent can hold back the codependent without learning trust. This is why it is so imperative for both people in the relationship to commit to changing behavior patterns and to stay on the path to recovery.

Establishing trust in one another supports the recovery process. The codependent trusts the dependent to handle their consequences, and the dependent trusts that the codependent will allow them the room to take responsibility on their own. As with any other process, establishing trust takes work, time, and patience. The dependent and codependent can't give up and let recovery fall by the wayside if they experience a setback in establishing trust.

With a strong bond of trust from the codependent, the dependent can learn personal behavior management. When the dependent sees evidence of the codependent's trust and faith in them, healing begins to move at a faster rate. As the codependent delegates more and more responsibility to the dependent, the dependent's confidence in themselves and their abilities grow. Even if the dependent experiences setbacks, having that confidence in themselves can help them move past the obstacle or mistake quickly and strengthen their resolve to return to the path of recovery as opposed to giving up. The codependent's trust is critical here.

Actually, setbacks and mistakes can further solidify trust. For example, if the dependent is a substance abuser and relapses, the codependent can take this as an opportunity to show their respect, love, and faith in the dependent by not falling back into their old behavior patterns and allowing the dependent to take responsibility for their actions while still being supportive. The codependent stays on the path to healing and the dependent can trust more deeply that the codependent will be there to help them instead of judging or controlling them. This will give the dependent (often overlooked) the assurance that the codependent will not abandon them for a mistake. This is not to say that the codependent should continue to allow setbacks to happen without consequence; the codependent needs to gauge the dependent's commitment to recovery. If the dependent backslides often and doesn't try and change their behavior, the codependent needs to assess the relationship and the likelihood that the dependent is actually trying to get out of their cycle of unhealthy behavior. As much as it may hurt, if the dependent is regularly holding the codependent back from healing, the two may find it better to part ways.

Once trust is established and solid, the codependent behaviors are further dissolved. Changing the codependent relationship has begun on a solid foundation of respect, communication, and trust.

Chapter 6: Breaking the Cycle of Codependency

Codependency is a cycle. In order to heal, the codependent and the dependent have to decide to break the cycle together. Both partners should work together to move forward. For the codependent that is not in a relationship or their dependent is unwilling to change or denies there is a problem, they can still move beyond the codependent behavior patterns as well.

The steps discussed so far that are required to break the cycle of codependency include being aware of and accepting the unhealthy codependent behaviors, staying mindful of yourself, your partner, and the relationship, setting boundaries, and accepting your partner. These are all hallmarks of healthy relationships.

Learning to put the codependent's needs first is a necessary step in the direction of breaking the cycle. The codependent is discovering healthy ways to fill the spaces a codependent relationship previously held, and they are also examining the root of the codependent behavior to work through the feelings their childhood left them with. As the codependent learns the reasons behind their unhealthy codependent needs, they will learn how to fill those needs in ways that leave them feeling whole instead of stressed and used.

In this chapter, healthy relationships and mindful relationship dynamics are examined. The dependent and codependent can see how their relationships can transform from unhealthy, codependence to a healthy, balanced relationship.

What does a healthy relationship look like?

It is a well-known fact that a codependent relationship is not a healthy one. Unfortunately, many dependent and codependent people have not ever had a good model of a healthy relationship. Codependent behavior is learned through observation and experience, so it stands to reason that a codependent has watched another codependent relationship as opposed to the healthy ones.

A codependent person is more focused on becoming the caretaker of their dependent than trying to observe healthy relationships, and then they fall into the cycle of cleaning up and handling their dependents' responsibility and decide that they don't have the energy to look around them. The codependent partner is not focusing on trying to make the relationship work because all of their energy is being used toward controlling the dependent and the relationship or trying to cover up for the dependent.

A healthy relationship consists of two people who want their partner to feel happy, are concerned about their well-being, and be physically healthy. Healthy relationships have conflict, a balance between compromising and meeting one another's needs, are able to be apart, and have a level of support and intimacy that is not controlling. Both people in the relationship have a sense of identity and independence, and though their partner is important to them, people in a healthy relationship don't base their entire being on the needs and emotions of each other.

A social life separate from the relationship is also a sign of a healthy relationship. The dependent and the codependent don't have to always be with one another, and in fact, time apart can strengthen the bond in the relationship. The codependent can become involved in things they are interested in or passionate about, and the time they previously spent in the relationship trying to change the dependent and manage the relationship can be spent in the new activities.

Relationships that are based on mutual respect are successful. Both people in the relationship have set boundaries and the other respects them. Neither partner feels as though they are responsible for the bulk of making the relationship work. One partner doesn't have to cover up or clean up for the other's behavior. Both partners take responsibility for working together to have a successful relationship.

Recovering from codependency requires a change from previous behaviors. Since many people, especially dependent people, won't recognize or respect the changes, the codependent person has to assert themselves and tell the people around them that they can no longer take advantage of them, and then they have to stick to that assertion when the dependents inevitably test the codependent's boundaries. Healthy relationships withstand those tests, even if they are difficult.

A person in a healthy relationship does not control their partner. A healthy relationship has partners who make suggestions for one another, but they don't force their partner to do what they want. Again, the person in a healthy relationship supports their partner.

Once the codependent person recognizes a healthy relationship, they begin to attract emotionally healthy people.

Maintaining a Mindful Relationship Dynamic

The codependent relationship has not used the principle of mindfulness. The codependent person may have developed a mindful practice but applying it to the relationship may not have occurred yet. Healthy relationships use mindfulness in interactions with one another. An emotionally healthy person is able to understand how to deal with conflict and is secure enough to know that they will not be abandoned during a conflict.

When mindfulness is used in relationships, it decreases stress on the relationship and encourages support and trust in one another. Learning mindfulness in a relationship means that both partners are conscious of their partner's needs. Mindfulness enables both partners to read one another's facial expressions and see what their partner is not saying aloud. Codependent people expect their partners to just *know* what they need without voicing it, but emotionally healthy partners know that even though their partner can sense some of their needs, they still need to let their partners know if they need something they're not getting.

Once a relationship begins working toward using mindfulness practices, maintaining them also takes work. Practicing mindfulness as an individual sets the groundwork for using it in relationships. Mindfulness opens up the acceptance each partner needs from the other. People in a healthy relationship accept themselves and their partners as they are. Accepting one another allows for conflict to be resolved easier, but it also signifies that the partners will not judge one another for their thoughts, feelings, and opinions. A healthy relationship with mindful partners allows each one to know that they are secure regardless of disagreements.

Keeping mindfulness as part of a healthy relationship keeps the relationship itself from spiraling into negativity.

Knowing When to Walk Away

Some major points in the codependent personality are being controlling, having the obsessive need to be right, having a fear of opening oneself up to vulnerability and being rejected, and frequently assuming responsibility for the dependent's actions. A codependent person relies on the need of the dependent person in order to feel validated. Over time, the codependent person feels trapped and unable to get the dependent person to do things for themselves. The codependent doesn't know when to walk away, say "no", or deny what the dependent wants.

Recovery from codependency teaches the codependent when they should walk away or assert boundaries for the dependent. The codependent must reach a point where they no longer have the capacity to help, but the demands of the dependent keep recurring. This is the point where boundaries must be set.

Unfortunately for the codependent, *they* must be the ones to set boundaries for the dependent. If the codependent doesn't set the boundary, the dependent will not make the association that the boundaries are legitimately something the codependent wishes to use. The codependent is responsible for setting the boundaries as well as enforcing them. If the codependent turns to an outside person, for example, a therapist, to set the boundary, they will never be able to set their own boundaries from then on out.

Only the codependent can decide when they've had enough from the dependent. It is also for this reason that the codependent can't look to someone else to outline the new boundaries for the dependent. The codependent is trying to move *away* from controlling or defeated behavior; asking someone to set boundaries for them has the opposite effect. Inevitably, the codependent will feel uncomfortable setting the boundary and then asserting it, but they must push past those feelings in order to overcome their codependent behavior. In addition to the codependent's expected discomfort, they must also understand that the dependent will be unhappy with the new restrictions. This is okay, enforcing boundaries facilitates trust and codependency recovery, and the certain pushback the codependent will face will also encourage the codependent's mindfulness, confidence, and offer them the opportunity to further their recovery.

Setting boundaries will help the codependent recognize where their "help" is no longer help and becomes more forceful or more enabling to the dependent's unhealthy behavior. The codependent will learn that it is okay to say "no" sometimes without guilt, and they will see that saying no, in fact, pushes the dependent in the direction of independence and their own recovery. The codependent must learn when to walk away from the dependent and the behaviors that initiate problems in the dependent's life. They must learn that they cannot fix everything and expect the dependent to learn from their mistakes or change.

Once the codependent learns where to draw the line, their path to recovery becomes well paved and less daunting.

Living the Life You Want to Live

By this point, the codependent has learned how to recognize, be aware, and accept their unhealthy behaviors. They have learned the importance of mindfulness, forgiveness, and setting boundaries. The path to recovery and healing has become easier with each step and with empathic listening and mutual respect, the codependent is learning how to cultivate a healthy relationship.

Healing in a codependent relationship encourages consistent learning. The more open a codependent is to frequent and steady education about themselves, their situation, and their healthier lives; the more likely they are to maintain an emotionally healthy lifestyle. There is always something new to learn about a healthy life. Permitting stagnation can lead back into codependent behavior patterns in the long run. Continuous reading and exposing themselves to other codependents in recovery encourages a stronger recovery for the codependent.

With these steps taken, the codependent is on their way to living a happier, emotionally healthy life. They are now able to pursue their own, real interests instead of what they think others want them to be interested in. The codependent is no longer codependent, but instead, they are now a more mindful, complete individual who doesn't have to base their entire being off one person or role. They can now feel complete with themselves as they are.

Being codependent isn't only missing out on what a healthy relationship has to offer. It also causes you to miss out on finding your own identity, your own passions. Being codependent causes you to miss out on true intimacy with someone - that feeling that someone in the world understands you, your needs, and accepts what you have to offer without conditions.

Codependency isn't something that necessarily has a permanent cure. Without vigilance and mindfulness, the codependent behaviors can once again appear and develop into patterns. However, that does not mean that you can't live the life you want, with the relationships you want. A recovering codependent is especially perceptive of unhealthy codependent behavior, so they are able to see instances when codependent behavior makes an appearance. When they pick up on codependent behavior, they have an opportunity to correct the behavior, so it won't get out of hand. Keeping the codependent behavior in check ensures that the recovering codependent can keep their healthy, full, and rich life.

Breaking the cycle of codependency leads to a more satisfying existence.

Conclusion

Thank you for making it through to the end of *Codependency: No more - The codependent recovery guide to cure wounded souls*. Let's hope it was informative and able to provide you with all of the tools you need to achieve your goals whatever they may be.

The next step is to begin to understand what codependent behaviors you exhibit and put the tips and information in this book into action. You may want to find help from a therapist, or even someone you can talk to that maybe has been in your shoes, with experience in overcoming the codependency you are feeling. Discussion forums, therapy hotlines, and even emailing with a therapist are a good place to start.

Understand that codependence is a life-long recovery process. You will experience setbacks and obstacles, and ultimately, you may find that the relationship you are in is not for you once you are undergoing the healing process. Your healing and recovery are the most important aspects here, and if you can summon the strength to stick with your path to recovery, you will be able to live your best life.

Thank you for reading! If you enjoyed this book, I would appreciate it if you went to the place of purchase and left a short positive review. Thank you